Programmed by God
or Free to Choose?

Programmed by God
or Free to Choose?

Five-Point Calvinism under the Searchlight

Dudley Ward

RESOURCE *Publications* · Eugene, Oregon

PROGRAMMED BY GOD OR FREE TO CHOOSE?
Five-Point Calvinism under the Searchlight

Resource Publications
A Division of Wipf and Stock Publishers
199 West 8th Avenue, Suite 3
Eugene, Oregon 97401

ISBN 13: 978-1-55635-391-8

Unless otherwise stated, Bible quotations are from the New King James Version, copyright © 1982 by Thomas Nelson, Inc., and New King James Version, Revised Edition, 1985. Additional relevant Scriptures for some chapters are given in the Appendix.

Manufactured in the U.S.A.

Contents

Acknowledgements

BOTH FRENCH AND ENGLISH-SPEAKING friends have offered me invaluable help in creating this book, and I have sought to express personally to each one my heartfelt gratitude. There are two people, however, who have particularly distinguished themselves in this respect. I would like to record my profoundest gratitude to Nancy Shoptaw for expertly improving and copyediting the manuscript far beyond my fondest hopes. Most of all, I want to pay unqualified tribute to my beloved wife, Jill, who has unstintingly supported me in this project and become my most invaluable production assistant.

—Melve
France
June 2008

Preface

THE FIVE-HUNDREDTH ANNIVERSARY OF John Calvin's birth occurs in 2009, and it seems appropriate to publish this book as we celebrate this very significant event.

As a young trainee teacher on summer vacation in France, the Lord Jesus Christ used an older missionary friend working there to redirect my life as a follower of Christ. Seven years later, after training in Canada, I assumed his responsibilities while he took a leave of absence in England to write a book warning of the dangers of spiritism. He had pioneered a little church in Aix-en-Provence in southeast France and wanted me to care for the congregation. I was also to continue visiting the open-air markets of the region with a portable book table displaying Bibles and Scripture extracts published in over twenty languages.

As a converted spiritist, he seemed well qualified to write on the topic. However, certain secret sins still beset him, and as he began writing, the enemy succeeded in persuading him that his failure to enjoy victory over such sins constituted proof that he had never been numbered amongst the elect and, consequently, had not been predestined to eternal life. Not even a visit from Dr. Martyn Lloyd-Jones, a well-known Welsh evangelical pastor and author, succeeded in dislodging this new mindset. Very soon afterwards, he died of personal neglect and starvation in a garret room. Those of us who knew him were left deeply distressed by the power of this false understanding.

I have come across many others desperately seeking an answer to the knotty question as to whether it is God's own predetermined choice alone that decrees who will be saved from eternal doom, or whether the genuine, free response to God of each individual has a crucial influence in the matter. This is my main reason for writing this book. I am not an Arminian of any shade. In fact, I have deliberately steered clear of any in-depth study of Jacob Arminius's written works, so that I might claim with integrity not to be directly influenced by his thought. Arminius (1560–1609), a Radical

Reformer, was not perceived to have a partisan spirit. He was brought up under the influence of Calvin's teaching, and most other Reformers acknowledged his spotless character and great learning. He made praiseworthy efforts to bring more balance into the Calvinist system, but sadly, went too far on some points; although he did not go to the same extremes as some of his followers after his death.

I wish also to state that I am not writing primarily for people who have had formal theological training. Other authors have already written competent and convincing rebuttals of the five main points of John Calvin's theological system as synthesized at the Council of Dordt (1618–19) and usually referred to as "TULIP." Definitions of the five points of TULIP theology are presented in the Introduction.

In attempting a brief survey, I am writing for very ordinary people who are troubled by TULIP teaching, that they might find release into a warmer and more intimate understanding of the true extent of the love of God in Christ. Let us never forget, however, that our degree of intimacy with the *Person* of Christ is even more important than our zeal in propagating our views on these matters.

By keeping the costs down, I hope that this book can be widely distributed among those who would most benefit from it. In an attempt to make it as complete, concise, simple, and direct as possible, I have chosen to stick with the Scriptures themselves as the main focus, rather than report what a multiplicity of authors have said on this matter. With general readers in mind, I wish to refer sparingly to supplemental resources, to hold footnotes to a minimum, and to quote few sources other than the Bible. The subject matter concerns Calvin's own statements, and within the text I have indicated their sources. However, very little of what I have stated is novel, simply because I am treating things similarly to the way the very early church fathers did, men who served the church before the time of Augustine of Hippo (354–430). This would include Christian leaders such as Iranaeus of Gaul, Athenagoras of Athens, Theophilus of Antioch, Tatian, Clement of Alexandria, Origen, Novatian of Rome, John Chrysostom, and Justin Martyr. Bible students should consider what these men actually wrote, rather than merely relying upon what those who were in disagreement said about them. This is also necessary concerning the much more recent writings of many devout Christians who disagree with some features of "Reformed" theology.

A word of caution needs to be added about equating the Reformation with either Martin Luther or John Calvin because, historically, other significant Christian streams were also involved. During the Reformation in the sixteenth century thousands of Bible-based believers throughout Europe belonged to movements such as the Anabaptists, and many had already distanced themselves from Roman Catholicism, and from any sponsorship of, or alliance with, State authorities. These faithful Christians, having abandoned adherence to the state church systems, had chosen to be associated with what historians now call the Radical Reformation. Their actions left a positive and abiding influence on subsequent generations.

You will notice that each chapter title in this book is phrased in the form of a question. We are in good company when we ask questions, as Jesus often used this method to stimulate the thinking of His hearers. We see this, for instance, in Mark 11:17 where it is said of Him, "He taught, saying to them, 'Is it not written . . . ?'" An important component of wisdom is knowing how to ask pertinent questions to the right people at the appropriate moment.

I am not claiming any originality, nor do I claim to have dealt exhaustively with all the relevant data. My goal is to present a kind, cogent, and concise alternative to Calvin's theological system by addressing the main issues, including the more difficult Scriptures relevant to the topic, while refraining from putting living authors in a bad light. Sadly, there are contemporary authors who, in countering TULIP theology, tend to run past some of the bases and treat with disrespect and belligerence those who disagree with them. I appeal to you, the reader, to discern for yourself whether in fact I have attained my desired goal of remaining kind to those whose views differ from my own.

Let us never forget that the development of the Spirit's fruit in us (see Galatians 5:22), notably love, kindness, and gentleness, should be more prominent than any aggressive fervor in promoting our own convictions.

I am willing to correspond with those requesting further help concerning the topics presented in this book. Feel free to write to me at: ambrosie3@gmail.com

Introduction

L ET ME INTRODUCE OUR reflections with a short story about three teen-agers. Bill, Ben, and Dave were looking for kicks, since they enjoyed getting into mischief. One day, just before a neighbor left for work, they decided to have fun by deflating one of the front tires on his car. Knowing that he would leave shortly for work, they then hid behind a hedge to watch. Soon the owner appeared, and suspecting nothing, jumped into his car and drove off. Further down the street a little girl was playing on the sidewalk, when suddenly her ball bounced away. Without thinking, she darted out into the path of the car. The driver, braking hard, swerved and lost control, injuring the little girl, slamming into a tree, and damaging himself and his car.

During the police inquiry, the evidence unmistakably showed that the deflated tire contributed to the accident, and that the lads were all equally responsible, having conspired together in their near-fatal interfer-ence with the neighbor's car. The judge considered it to have been a par-ticularly dangerous prank for which all three young men, being equally guilty, needed to be punished in order to learn a lesson. None of them had ever before been in trouble with the police, and they felt terrible about the whole thing. However, the judge announced that he would let Bill go free, but would sentence Ben and Dave to two months of community service. What would be your reaction to a judge who passed sentence in this manner?

This story exemplifies the recurrent problem of injustices encoun-tered in everyday life. God certainly permits all sorts of things to happen that we feel we could well do without, and we have to remind ourselves that He, who is wholly righteous in every aspect of His being, always acts with perfect justice. Generally speaking, even most non-Christians have a keen sense of justice, so why would God's perfect justice seem to conflict in any way with a committed child of God's acute sense of right and wrong? Yet most Calvinists believe that the *determining* factor in the salvation of a specific individual is God's sovereign choice, as they understand it, either to bestow on that person, or to withhold from him, His grace and pardon according to His own good pleasure. This granting of grace, in their eyes, would be without taking into account the sinner's own genuine desire, or lack of it, for communion with God. Calvin even maintained that at the Fall, man lost all desire for God.

A tenet of John Calvin's doctrinal system, known by the acronym TULIP subsequent to the deliberations of the Council of Dordrecht (Dordt) in Holland, says emphatically that if a person ends up in hell, it is primarily because God chose this destination for him before he was born. This means that God decided in advance "to pass him over," refusing him the necessary graces of repentance, forgiveness, and the gift of eternal life that would make it possible for him to escape such a fate by freely turning to God. Calvinists say that this supposed divine choice glorifies God. Therefore, as Calvin understood it, before time began God decided to deprive certain individuals of any opportunity to receive eternal life.

In addition, Calvin taught that everything that happens on earth, however sinful and vile, is the result of God's specific plan and purpose, and the expression of His will. He saw this as being distinct from the fact that God *can know* everything in advance, including how our bad choices will affect His perfect plans. Calvin also stated that God planned and willed the Fall of man.

The Calvinist party convened the Council of Dordt in 1618–19 in order to set out systematically what they perceived to be John Calvin's understanding of soteriology—the doctrine of salvation. They considered it the only teaching faithful to the Scriptures, and they also sought to obtain a basic mandate for dealing with dissent. The Council of Dordt, although it took place in the same town in Holland, Dordrecht, is not to be confused with the Dordrecht Confession of Faith of 1632, a significant landmark in Mennonite history.

Here, defined by Calvinists themselves, and taken from various translated sources, are the five points that summarize the conclusions of the Council of Dordt:

1. **Total Depravity or Total Inability:** Because of the Fall of man in the Garden of Eden, man is unable of himself to believe upon the Lord Jesus Christ for salvation. The sinner is dead, blind, and deaf to the things of God. His heart is deceitful and desperately

corrupt. His will is not free, for it is in bondage to his evil nature. Therefore, he will not—indeed he cannot—choose good over evil in the spiritual realm. Consequently, it takes much more than the Spirit's assistance to bring a sinner to Christ. It takes regeneration, by which the Spirit makes the sinner alive, and gives him a new nature that will enable him to believe upon the Lord Jesus. Faith is not something man contributes to salvation, but is itself a part of God's gift of salvation. It is God's gift to the sinner, not the sinner's gift to God. Of himself, man cannot even desire to seek God.

2. **Unconditional Election:** God's choice of certain individuals unto salvation, before the foundation of the world, resided solely in His own sovereign will. Therefore, He did not base His choice of particular sinners on any foreseen response of obedience on their part, such as faith or repentance. On the contrary, God grants faith and repentance only to the individuals whom He has previously selected; and faith and repentance are the results, not the cause, of God's choice. Therefore, "election unto salvation" is not determined by, or dependent upon, any virtuous quality or act foreseen in man. God brings to a willing acceptance of Christ, through the power of the Spirit, those whom He has sovereignly elected. Thus God's choice of a particular sinner, not that sinner's choice of Christ, is the sole agent in salvation.

3. **Limited Atonement:** In His redeeming work, Christ intended to save only the elect, and actually secured salvation for them alone. His death, the substitutionary payment for the penalty of sin, was only for certain specified sinners. In addition to putting away the sins of His people, Christ's redemption secured everything necessary for their salvation, including the faith that unites them to Him. The Spirit applies the gift of faith only and unfailingly to those thus chosen to be the beneficiaries of Christ's death, thereby assuring their salvation.

4. **Irresistible Grace or the Efficacious Call of the Spirit:** In addition to the outward and general call to salvation which is made to everyone who hears the gospel, the Holy Spirit extends to the elect a special inward call that unfailingly brings them to salvation. Those who are not the elect reject the external

call, made to all without distinction, whereas the internal call, addressed only to the elect, cannot be rejected. It always results in salvation. By means of this special call, the Spirit irresistibly draws sinners to Christ. He is neither limited by man's will in His work of applying salvation, nor is He dependent upon man's cooperation for success. The Spirit graciously causes the elect sinner to cooperate, to believe, to repent, and to come freely and willingly to Christ. Therefore God's grace is invincible, never failing to result in the salvation of those to whom He extends it.

5. **Perseverance of the Saints:** Salvation is accomplished by the almighty power of the triune God. The Father chose a people, the Son died for them, and the Holy Spirit makes Christ's death effective by bringing the elect to faith and repentance through a sovereign act of regeneration that causes them willingly to obey the gospel. The entire process of election and regeneration, resulting in full redemption and eternal security, is exclusively the work of God and is by grace alone.

Returning to the first of the five points of TULIP, here is a translated sentence from the Council of Dordt, Article 3, Section 3:

> All men are conceived in sin and are born as children of wrath, incapable of anything good, bent towards evil, dead in sin and slaves of sin. Without regenerating grace they do not want to (nor are they able to) turn to God, neither can they correct their depraved nature nor even desire to change it.[1]

In the above quote, one could easily miss the emergence of the idea that regeneration precedes both the desire to seek God and the ability to put one's trust in Jesus Christ. Yet Romans 2:4 speaks of God's kindness leading us specifically to repentance rather than to regeneration. I seek to demonstrate in chapter 7 that repentance is neither dependent upon, nor a result of, regeneration, but a disposition of spirit that leads to it.

Here is how the Westminster Confession—a later formulation of Calvinist doctrine in England, and part of the Westminster Standards adopted in 1647 under King Charles 1—described the universal result of the Fall:

1. *Dordt*, http://www.reformed.org/documents/canons_of_dordt.html, lines 1–2.

From this original corruption, whereby we are utterly indisposed, disabled and made opposite to all good, and wholly inclined to all evil, do proceed all actual transgressions.

Does this extract from the articles of the Westminster Confession of Faith accurately describe our own experience of how unsaved people consistently behave? Is every unsaved person in your life "wholly inclined to all evil"? I will explain later the particular usage Paul gives to the quote in Romans 3:10 from Psalm 36. Those of us who have been through wars know what noble and heroic deeds are sometimes accomplished. Soldiers are known to choose to die in an attempt to protect their comrades. One needs to ask if both Calvin's and the Westminster Confession's descriptions of human behavior are not less than accurate. I will endeavor to show both that they reveal poor theology concerning this topic and that they contradict common everyday facts.

Neighbors often do good things for one another without any claim to having been regenerated by God's Holy Spirit. In order to keep their view of God's sovereignty intact, TULIP proponents are inclined to put man's fallen nature in the worst possible light, while highlighting the sublimely sovereign nature of God. Of course, God's holiness, kindness, and goodness far transcend our human ability to describe, but nowhere does the Bible (taken as a whole) portray all men in TULIP's lugubrious terms. Let us remember always that Cornelius could be counted much like the Centurion in the Gospels, as both were described as men who feared God, and acted charitably before ever receiving Jesus into their life. The men who assembled to hear and receive Peter's testimony, as recorded in Acts chapter 2, are also described as devout men, even before their conversion. (See Luke 7:4–5; Acts 2:2; and Acts 10:2–4.)

How urgent it is for us all to return to a balanced biblical view of mankind's sinful condition! With this is mind, let us remember that the New Testament does not negate in any way the moral teaching and comments found in the Old Testament; they are altogether complementary.

We find a very clear passage describing the behavior of wicked people in Psalm 10. We know that the main theme of this Psalm is not, in fact, the universal condition of sinful man, for it refers to the humble in verse 17, and the fatherless and oppressed in verse 18. However, these people are not the focus of the Psalm. It is specifically about the behavior of wicked people, not about that of humanity in general. Do all the unsaved people in your life bless the greedy, persecute the poor, and fill their mouth with cursing, deceit, and oppression, with trouble and iniquity under their tongue? Here we read a detailed description of the type of person who does not seek God, and who chooses to renounce Him (vss.4, 13), as distinct from the many who are ignorant of the possibility of a personal relationship with Him. Why would the psalmist even refer to the fact that such wicked people do not seek God, if such absence of seeking were the universal characteristic of all mankind? Let us meditate upon this Psalm and ask ourselves whether the first tenet of TULIP concerning total depravity conforms to these words of Scripture.

Some Calvinist theologians want us to discern a difference between *total* depravity and *utter* depravity, but both Webster's and the Oxford dictionaries confirm that these two words are synonymous. In order to express the subtleties of TULIP theology, special definitions seem to have been devised by some of its chief contemporary exponents! Theology, like history, can become very subjective. How hard it is for us all to resist searching within the pages of Scripture for support for our own preconceived notions!

The evangelical world seems to be afflicted by deep disagreement over the extent of Christ's atoning work. The gospel says that Jesus died for the sins of all mankind without exception, and yet many Christians would deny this! They say that He only died for those chosen by God before time began. This book sets out to determine which of these two views faithfully represents the *good news* presented within the pages of Scripture. It also seeks to demonstrate that man is indeed a fallen creature, but that he is not always "wholly inclined to all evil." The fact that he sins at all is sufficient to make him need the atoning work of the Lord Jesus on his behalf, as does his being a member of the fallen human race. According to Romans 3:23, "*All* have sinned and come short of the glory of God" (italics mine). Falling short of God's glory is very different from all having inevitably become "utterly corrupt in every part."

Article 6 of the Council of Dordt states:

> The fact that some receive the gift of faith from God, while others do not receive it, proceeds from God's eternal decree, according to which decree He graciously softens the hearts of the elect, however

obstinate, while He leaves the non-elect in this just judgment to their own wickedness and obduracy.[2]

We find the following in Article 7:

> Election is the unchangeable purpose of God whereby, before the foundation of the world, He has, out of mere grace, according to the sovereign good pleasure of His own will, chosen from the whole human race ... a certain number of persons to redemption in Christ ...[3]

The apostle Paul emphasizes how essential it is that we put our faith in the living God, rather than in theological systems. He does so by discouraging the use of any defining label apart from "of Christ" or "Christian." Let us take note of his words in 1 Corinthians 1:12: "Now I say this, that each of you says, 'I am of Paul,' or 'I am of Apollos,' or 'I am of Cephas,' or 'I am of Christ.'" It is plainly unscriptural to identify oneself exclusively with any specific historic theological system, including that of Calvin. If one has sought to walk with God for many years, especially with all the added benefits of modern scholarship available today, could not one's grasp of God's character and dealings with man be as good as John Calvin's, or even better when one considers the limitations of his epoch? Why is there this widespread inner compulsion to claim mere human support for one's convictions? Cannot each person be his own man, and if necessary, stand alone and tall on the solid foundation of Scripture's plain statements?

Paul seems to indicate that it would be equally wrong for us to put labels on other saints or to group people together, sometimes grossly mis-representing their lives and beliefs. History offers us many examples of such disreputable behavior having greatly contributed to division in the church; yet invective seems to continue unabated.

However, since thousands of our beloved fellow-believers do indeed identify themselves as Calvinists, I will use that term in this book, and attempt to show that amongst so much that is excellent in John Calvin's teachings, the five points of TULIP have been constructed on a very questionable foundation. Having said that, it is certainly true that some

2. *Dordt*, http://www.reformed.org/documents/canons_of_dordt.html, lines 1–2.

3. *Dordt*, http://www.reformed.org/documents/canons_of_dordt.html, lines 1–2.

Calvinists are, in practice, much closer to spiritual truth than he was on some points. We need to note that not all who call themselves Calvinists subscribe to all five points of TULIP doctrine.

Who Were John Calvin and Some of His Contemporaries?

B ORN IN 1509 IN Picardy, France, John Calvin was greatly impressed as a young man by the calm way in which a Christian martyr faced death at the stake. In about 1527, he left Roman Catholicism, and sometime later experienced the new birth. Very insecure political and social conditions eventually caused him to flee to Switzerland. There in 1536, when Calvin was aged twenty-seven, the first edition of his *Institutes of the Christian Religion* was published in Basle, just nine years after he had left Roman Catholicism. Although it originally comprised only six chapters written in Latin, Calvin greatly enlarged the work over the next twenty-four years, and it was soon translated into French and subsequently into English.

Calvin's desire to create a "holy commonwealth" was in part fulfilled in Geneva. By then the city had thrown off the authority of both the Roman Catholic bishop and the duke of neighboring Savoy. The Swiss town of Bern, recently won over to the Reformation, had helped in this, but Geneva itself had not yet become a member of the Swiss Confederation. By the treaty of February 1544, during Calvin's tenure, Geneva became for a time an independent entity to which gospel ministers from France fled, seeking shelter from persecution.

William Farel, from Gap, in southeast France, an ardent preacher of righteousness, had unwittingly brought the population of Geneva to the verge of civil war before the magistrates hastily restored order by acceding to some elements of reform. However, for all his forcefulness, Farel felt unequal to the task of following through on fully reforming the city, and when young Calvin was passing through, Farel pressed him into service by threats of severe censure if he declined. Calvin capitulated.

Calvin's own convictions on the relations between church and state soon led to more friction. He rightly and persistently maintained that the church itself was meant to be independent, and that it alone could determine what form liturgical matters should take. Above all else, he affirmed that only the church had the right to excommunicate uncooperative souls. The magistrates resisted this latter assertion, and Calvin was briefly banished from Geneva to Strasbourg because of his insistence. Nevertheless, he was recalled in 1541 and, after another brief tussle in 1553, the point was finally conceded that ecclesiastical discipline should be exercised by the church and not by the civil authorities.

Even so, the city council, which tended to wage a continual war of wits with Calvin, possessed extensive powers in civil and religious matters. Calvin assumed that every member of the city-state of Geneva was also under the discipline of the church, and citizens were required to sign a confession of faith or leave the city.

When Servetus, a medical doctor whose religious views differed radically from those of Calvin, was put on trial elsewhere and imprisoned by the Roman Catholic hierarchy, he escaped and was later recognized as he passed through Geneva. Calvin ordered his arrest and he was put on trial, convicted, and burned at the stake with the approval of both Calvin and other Reformers. Servetus denied the divinity of the Holy Spirit, and said that Jesus was not the eternal Son. A highly intelligent but pugnacious man, who could also be explosive, vitriolic, and offensive with those who disagreed with his theology, he nevertheless did good research in the medical field. He is credited for having traced the circulation of the blood twenty-five years before William Harvey did so. Writing voluminously on religious topics, he attacked Calvin with vicious abuse, accusing him of being "a liar, a fool, a cheat, and a scoundrel." We can sympathize with Calvin's desire to get rid of him!

No one can deny Calvin's intellectual greatness or his tireless work in seeking to reform the Church. He lived frugally in selfless devotion to what he believed to be the will of God. His mother had died when he was only six years old. In 1540, Calvin married Idelette, a widow with two children. Early in their marriage the couple lost three children, two having been born prematurely and the third dying in infancy. Then, after only nine years together, Idelette died, probably of tuberculosis, when Calvin was just forty years old.

Calvin remained French, never becoming a citizen of Geneva. He could be temperamentally unpredictable, often showing gentleness and compassion toward others, but at other times being coarse and angry, especially with those who disagreed with his theology. His frequent and painful health problems undoubtedly affected his disposition.

Calvin had an intriguingly restricted view of congregational singing. His recommendation was to "sing psalms, simply, with no harmony." Was this one more indication of his austere and solemn temperament? He maintained this attitude towards music in church, although there were many gifted and devout composers of his epoch who wrote wonderfully harmonious church music based on Scripture.

After his sermons, Calvin would customarily bid the congregation to fall down before God's majesty, asking Him to grant grace both to them and to all peoples on earth. He invited them to do this in spite of having written that there were people on earth whom God had no desire or intention of saving.

Calvin, at the age of fifty-five and aware of his approaching death, met for the last time with his fellow ministers. He was by then very frail and unable to get out of bed, but clear in mind. He passed under review his long ministry in Geneva, expressing himself in a strange mixture of devotion, self-justification, and bitterness. Part of what he communicated to the fellow ministers gathered around his sickbed, included regrets that he felt his efforts had been worth nothing and that he was a miserable creature. He maintained that he had wanted to accomplish great things but that his shortcomings had always clung to him. He then declared, significantly, that he had not falsified a single passage of Scripture, nor had he, to the best of his knowledge, interpreted it wrongly. Most significant of all, he stated that changes were dangerous and sometimes harmful. Why did he say this? Was he reluctant to bring into focus, and seriously question, his own understanding of the exact nature of God's sovereignty, election to salvation, grace, predestination, and free will? Could he have been resisting a growing awareness that his position on election was flawed after all? Are all changes by nature harmful? Are we witnessing here a certain intellectual rigidity that overrides willingness to change? Was he strongly emphasizing the old nature, described in Romans chapter 7, without exulting in the Spirit's liberating and transforming work described in Romans chapter 8? Paul exulted in being seated in heavenly places in Christ (see Ephesians 2:6), and there is a note of great triumph in his conscious enjoyment of an unfading heavenly inheritance. It would seem tragic if Calvin, after all the trials he endured, failed to rejoice in the assurance of his Savior's closeness and the rewards and bliss that undoubtedly awaited him in heaven.

Nobody would deny that our experiences tend to color our view of God. Who would question, having studied human behavior, the role that temperament tends to play in our religious preferences? The tragic losses of affection and poor health that Calvin experienced may partly explain his spiritual austerity. For years he suffered from insomnia, digestive troubles, and bleeding hemorrhoids. Towards the end of his life, he also developed painful kidney stones, ejecting several through the urinary canal, tearing it in the process. We must acknowledge and honor Calvin's perseverance and dogged devotion to what he felt called to accomplish in spite of severe suffering.

During just twenty-four years of intensive spiritual ministry, Calvin succeeded in writing more than forty-five published books, including his commentaries on many books of the Bible, his three volumes of tracts, and what is considered to be his crowning achievement, *Institutes of the Christian Religion*. He died in poverty in 1564.

In his written works Calvin was seldom tender towards those who disagreed with him. Over a thousand years earlier, Augustine of Hippo (354–430), had recommended that those who had been baptized as infants, and who sought to be rebaptized as believers, be put to death. Neither Calvin nor Luther are recorded as having said anything to discourage the vicious persecution in Switzerland, Germany, France, Holland, and elsewhere of thousands of participants in the Radical Reformation. This parallel movement, although in some regions guilty of excesses, generally sought a complete return to all of the faith and practice revealed in the New Testament. They believed in the separation of church and state, and accepted for baptism only those who made a confession of faith in the Lord Jesus and His atoning work.

It was Augustine who, by his misinterpretation of the parable in Luke 14:16–23, introduced the notion of forcing people into God's kingdom. Verse 23 speaks of compelling people to come and fill the banquet hall. Augustine also formulated the views on predestination that Calvin later adopted. There is no doubt at all that Calvin was more heavily influenced by Augustine, whom he very frequently quotes, than by any other earlier church leaders.

Meanwhile, the Radical Reformation had been under way long before the Reformation itself took root in Europe. Most Radical Reformers within Europe were dubbed "Anabaptists" (rebaptized), and included Christian streams that became known as Mennonites, Amish, Hutterites, and the Churches of the Brethren. Their principles usually included no coercion in matters of religious belief, and they practiced believers' baptism by immersion or by pouring water over the candidate. Theirs was a simple lifestyle, and they emphasized a daily outworking of practical sanctification as well as what Calvinists called "forensic justification," forensic referring to our legal standing before God. This means that once we are "in Christ," we are declared righteous, even though our everyday behavior may still leave much to be desired. The sixteenth-century Radical Reformers emphasized the fact that both of these aspects need to be worked out in the lives of believers.

The Anabaptists focused on practical Christian living rather than on creeds and confessions of doctrinal belief. For them, spiritual reality was solely anchored on the solid rock of biblical truth under the daily guiding authority of the Holy Spirit. Also numbered amongst them were pacifists and those who rejected formal theological training.

John Calvin devoted no less than thirty-six pages in chapter 16 of his *Institutes of the Christian Religion* to defending and promoting in a most forthright way the baptism of infants, teaching that it is a New Testament rite that functions similarly to Old Testament circumcision. Sadly, in dealing with this topic, he allows for no differing opinion. Is it not intriguing that some Christian streams that vigorously oppose infant baptism today should nevertheless call themselves Calvinists? Many believers are ill informed, and are satisfied with just secondary sources as their authority in matters of religious truth. Go to Calvin, thou sluggard (see Proverbs 6:6), and study what the great man really had to say! You will find an abundance of excellent things that he taught, as well as some big surprises.

Both civil authorities and Reformed churches (that is to say Calvinistic and Lutheran) viewed Anabaptists as dangerous and heretical people. However, dozens of reliable historical documents attest to the fact that, in all major areas of Christian belief, most Anabaptists were indeed faithful followers of the Lord Jesus Christ, and should not have been judged as heretical. Thousands were hunted down and executed, including women and children. Many young children were taken from their parents and raised by loyal members of the official state churches. Finally, the violent persecution by Calvinists and other Reformers of those who disagreed with their convictions became so intense that waves of emigration began.

These led to the founding of colonies such as Plymouth in Massachusetts in 1620, less than one year after the closure of the Council of Dordt. At that time the Speedwell, a ship that soon linked up with the Mayflower, set sail from Delft Haven, Holland, carrying English-speaking expatriates, including Calvinists and Reformers of a more tolerant bent, all of whom sought to escape religious bigotry, dogmatism, and oppression.

Menno Simons (1496–1561), the father of the Mennonites, had been a Roman Catholic priest. When the authorities executed his brother, Peter, along with three hundred other Anabaptists seeking shelter from persecution in his hometown in Holland, Menno was profoundly moved by their shining testimony. Thus began a period of deep questioning, doubt, searching, and pleading with God, which he described as follows:

> My heart trembled in my body. I prayed to my God, with sighs and tears that He would grant the gift of His grace to me a troubled sinner, create in me a clean heart, through the efficacy of the blood of Christ forgive my unclean walk and vain gross life, and give to me wisdom, spirit, courage, and manly heroism so that I might preach genuinely His worshipful high Name and His holy Word and bring to light His truth unto His praise.[1]

Years later, writing of his conversion experience, Menno said that he was willing to renounce his worldly reputation, name, fame, and comfortable existence; and was ready to submit to a life of poverty and distress for the sake of Christ. He also rejected infant baptism.

An important contemporary of Menno Simons was Balthazar Hübmaier who was born in 1481, and cruelly burned at the stake in Vienna in 1528. After serving as a Roman Catholic priest, he decided to trust in Christ alone for his salvation, and to walk in obedience to Him, producing some valuable written statements of Radical Reformation conviction. Zwingli, another well-known Reformer, had him arrested and stretched on the rack, which *persuaded* him to sign a confession of heresy. This was a serious setback for Hübmaier, but he soon repented of having signed the confession, and zealously continued to serve the Lord Jesus Christ. Balthazar Hübmaier and Menno Simons both possessed the cour-

---

1. Broadbent, *Pilgrim Church*, 188.

age and insight to seek to implement some New Testament truths that the more prominent Reformers chose to disregard. *Sola Scriptura* (upholding Scripture itself as the only authority in matters of faith and conduct) was nowhere taken to heart more seriously than amongst most of the despised Anabaptists.

In his commentary on Genesis 3:6, Calvin says:

> Because of the Fall, we are born vicious and perverse . . . That we are lost and condemned and subjected to death, is both our heredi- tary condition and at the same time a just punishment which God, in the person of Adam, has inflicted upon the human race.[2]

Is there not something to question in this quotation? Did Adam's sin mean that we are all lost and condemned because of it? Alternatively, is it our own sin that makes us guilty before God, or is it both Adam's and ours? We all die physically because of the Fall, but are we condemned spiritually uniquely because of Adam's sin? Is it not our own freely chosen yielding to sinful desires that needs forgiveness and cleansing? Job was referred to as "blameless." How could Job, even if he walked uprightly, and he did, be called blameless, if he was nevertheless guilty because of the Fall? The New Testament exhorts us all to be blameless, but would such an encouragement make sense if we all carry blame for Adam's sin? The truth is that the cross of Christ placed all humans on a fundamental basis of redemption. However, to find out what is so misleading in some of Calvin's statements, we will move on through the themes developed in the following chapters, and marvel at the tender loving-kindness of God.

It is not my purpose in this short book to cover every unconvincing or inconsistent point that occurs in Calvin's writings, amidst so much that is admirable, but as we take a fresh look at TULIP topics, we can aim for a balanced biblical perspective concerning the true nature of God's sov- ereignty and our freedom of choice. Our love of God's Word should wean us from reliance on men's opinions, and allow all of Scripture to speak to our hearts. The choice is constantly before us. Either we come in humil- ity and openness to all of God's Word in its plain meaning, or we allow men's opinions to compromise its impact and influence our outlook. Of course, this is not to say that we can close our hearts to what God might want to teach us through the practical and significant spiritual wisdom of others, including Calvin himself. However, what we hear and receive must

2. Calvin, *Genesis*, 153–55.

be compared with *all* of Scripture, and be in total harmony with it, as we study these topics prayerfully and in dependence upon the Holy Spirit.

When some of the Pilgrim Fathers set sail in the *Speedwell* from Delft Haven in Holland, John Robinson, an English preacher, addressed them in these solemn tones:

> I charge you before God and His blessed angels, that you follow further than you have seen me follow the Lord Jesus Christ. If God reveals anything to you by any other instrument of His, be as ready to receive it as you were to receive any truth in my ministry, for I am verily persuaded the Lord hath more truth yet to break forth out of His Holy Word. For my part, I cannot sufficiently bewail the condition of those reformed churches which . . . will go no further than the instruments of their reformation . . . The Calvinists, you see, stick fast where they were left by that great man of God, who yet saw not all things. This is a misery much to be lamented, for though they were burning and shining lights in their times, yet they penetrated not into the whole counsel of God. Were they now living, they would be as willing to embrace further light as that which they first received, for it is not possible the Christian world should come so lately out of such thick anti-Christian darkness and that perfection of knowledge should break forth at once.[3]

The Anabaptist spirit is woven into the matrix of contemporary church life, there where religious freedom and separation of church and state are prized. Many Calvinists today tend to enjoy this light and liberty without giving credit to their true historical precedent. Jesus categorically said that He would build *His* church and that the gates of hell would not prevail against it. (See Matthew 16:18.) John Nelson Darby (1800–1882), prominent in the Plymouth Brethren movement, taught that the church was in ruins. This contradicted both Jesus' statement and the evidence that ever since Pentecost there has been a strong thread of theological integrity and New Testament practice in the world, which was preserved intact throughout the Reformation period. The New Testament itself, not creeds or pamphlets, remained the authority and guide for thousands whose faith-filled exploits are forever recorded in heaven. Incidentally, John Darby, who appeared to agree with TULIP thinking, fell out with D. L. Moody, who always championed man's ability as a responsible person to respond freely to God.

---

3. Broadbent, *Pilgrim Church*, 245–46.

Pertinent Scriptures for further reading include: James 3:17; 1 Thessalonians 2:7; Titus 3:2; 2 Corinthians 10:1; and Galatians 5:22–23.

2

Is Predestination a Mystery?

MANY CHRISTIANS HAVE BEEN taught that the doctrines of predestination and genuine human freedom of choice are irreconcilable "mysteries" in the current sense of the word. Webster gives as the prime meaning of predestination: "The act by which God supposedly preordained everything that would happen."[1]

We read of the mystery of faith and of godliness in 1 Timothy 3:9 and 16, and Paul also speaks of iniquity as a mystery in 2 Thessalonians 2:7. However, we also read of "The mystery that has been hidden from ages and from generations, but *now has been revealed* to his saints. To them God *willed to make known* what are the riches of the glory of this mystery among the Gentiles: which is Christ in you, the hope of glory" (Col 1: 26–27; italics mine). The same thought is repeated by the apostle Paul, who tells us that God has revealed to us things concerning His will that previously remained hidden: "*having made known to us the mystery of His will*, according to His good pleasure which He purposed in Himself, that in the dispensation of the fullness of the times He might gather together in one all things in Christ" (Eph 1:9–10; italics mine). The Greek word for "mystery" in these contexts refers to truth revealed as distinct from truth concealed. These verses make it plain that, in Christ, God wants to reveal, not hide, the mystery of the gospel, as does Ephesians 6:19: "And pray for me, that utterance may be given to me, that I may open my mouth boldly *to make known* the mystery of the gospel" (italics mine).

Paul wrote, "how that by revelation He made known to me the mystery (as I have briefly written already by which, when you read, you may understand my knowledge in the mystery of Christ), which in other ages was not made known to the sons of men, as it has now been revealed by

---

1. *Webster's*, 1149.

the Spirit to His holy apostles and prophets that the Gentiles should be fellow heirs of the same body, and partakers of His promise in Christ through the gospel" (Eph 3:3–6). He continued, "and to make all [not just 'some'!] see what is the fellowship of the mystery, which from the beginning of the ages has been hidden in God who created all things through Jesus Christ; to the intent that now the manifold wisdom of God might be made known by the church to the principalities and powers in the heavenly places" (Eph 3:9).

The New Testament seeks to clarify, not to mystify, the gospel! Are not predestination and authentic human freedom of choice both part of "the mystery of the gospel" and integral components of God's redemptive plan? Since the Bible nowhere presents predestination as something that continues to be mysterious and hidden, what would now be the point of mystifying this basic truth of the gospel? (See also Ephesians 3:2–6 and 9–10.) Again, let us note in all these references the recurrent phrase, "make known the mystery of the gospel."

Paul never attempted to relegate predestination, election, choice, or free will to the realm of hidden things. Nevertheless, Calvin maintained that God not only had a "revealed" will, but also a "secret" will, which was different from, and could even contradict, His declared will. Let me assure you straight away that God does not have a second, secret will that acts independently of, and can be at variance with, His revealed will. Paul knew that we could always trust our heavenly Father to be totally straight and up-front with His children.

We recognize, however, that there indeed are secrets that God the Father enjoys with His Son and with the Holy Spirit; and various other secrets were kept from His Son, certainly by His own choice, while on earth. For instance, in Matthew 24:36 we are told that Jesus Himself did not know the exact time of His own future return to earth. In counseling situations, some secrets have to be kept forever. God Himself is in no way obligated to reveal precious secrets. We can be sure, though, that our promotion to heaven's glory will inaugurate a process of learning things so wonderful that we could never have even dreamt of them while we remained earthbound.

God does sometimes choose to reveal secrets to His choice servants, and in the book of Daniel we read how God told Daniel things he could not possibly know by observation or deduction, such as Nebuchadnezzar's dream of future events. In a night-time vision, Daniel received a revelation from the Holy Spirit that showed him clearly, and in full detail, what had been going on in the king's mind. "There is a God in heaven who reveals secrets, and He has made known to King Nebuchadnezzar what will be in the latter days. Your dream, and the visions of your head upon your bed, were these" (Dan 2:28). Daniel then proceeds to relate to the king the exact contents of his supernatural dream.

When we come to the New Testament epistles, it is intriguing to discover that God's secrets are very much played down. Why? A new era had begun. God had accomplished redemption in space and time, and His plan was now being fully and wonderfully revealed.

Our heavenly Father has every desire to reveal to us His majestic compassionate plan to reach the lost. All that we need to understand concerning the whole strategy of redemption, including predestination, election, foreknowledge, and free will, is not concealed, but rather is unveiled within the pages of the New Testament. God never meant these facets of His redemptive activity to be conundrums, seeming contradictions, or insoluble puzzles.

Calvin taught that in order for God to be fully glorified, He "passes over" all the "non-elect," and purposes that they all justly endure His righteous wrath in hell as due punishment for their sins. Could any "Christian" idea be less charitable or accurate than the notion that, by "passing over them," God consequently wills people inevitably and irremediably to remain in unbelief and go to hell? The Lord takes no pleasure at all in the death of the wicked and in wickedness, as noted in Ezekiel 33:11: "Say unto them: 'As I live, says the Lord God, I have no pleasure in the death of the wicked, but that the wicked turn from his way and live. Turn, turn from your evil ways, for why should you die, O house of Israel?'"

Conscious that we must guard against taking illustrations too far, we could think of predestination in terms of a railroad service. A teenager is leaving Chicago for a visit with friends in Cincinnati. His mother has helped pack his suitcase and given him a nice bagged lunch. The railroad authorities have fixed the destination of the train and published the timetable. Leaving Chicago before lunch and reaching Cincinnati mid-afternoon, after a stop at Indianapolis, the train, which is entirely non-smoking, will include a restaurant car. Parental love and kindness help the teenager towards the goal, but the railroad authorities fix the train schedule and facilities months in advance. The young person, however, still has to make the final move, to choose to buy a ticket and get on the right train.

The railroad's authority ("sovereignty") is in no way lessened by the options that its clients will choose, for it has "predestined" such options in the public interest. The young man freely chooses to board the right train. During the journey, he is able to leave his seat at will, walk up and down the corridor, and visit the buffet and restroom; while all the time the train is speeding on to its fixed destination. The young man has no thought of congratulating himself for buying the ticket and boarding the train. There is no personal merit involved.

I will attempt to demonstrate that God has already done everything to help deliver all people from sin, short of violating their freedom of choice. He hates all sin and is totally opposed to it. However, having done all that is necessary to deliver every sinner, God is not coercive. Sins are primarily human choices rather than something programmed by God, as Calvin would have us believe. Enlightened societies have customarily held criminals responsible for their acts, and the desire is that after prisoners are released from their term of punishment, they begin a new life of usefulness. Good human justice seeks this change of heart, so why, in complete contrast, would God remove all possibility of a changed life? The hope of a change of heart is always there. Would it be in keeping with His character, as revealed in the Lord Jesus, to punish a person for continuing in his sins if He had held out no possible hope of change and redemption?

Let us stop and consider the following grave concept. A baby born through no choice of his own, with a sin nature he did not choose to inherit, will, one day, inevitably sin against God. According to Calvin, God may have decided, before this particular baby's birth, that he would be marked out for eternity in hell, and therefore He would have chosen to do nothing to meet the child's need of forgiveness and deliverance. This means that if indeed the eternal destiny of each one depended on God alone, newborn babies who die in infancy could be consigned to hell without having had an opportunity to do anything at all personally to deserve it. Would our all-loving God have created some people for the expressed purpose of torturing them forever?

Speaking of His impending death, Jesus uses an illustration from childbirth in these terms: "A woman, when she is in labor, has sorrow because her hour has come; but as soon as she has given birth to the child, she no longer remembers the anguish, for joy that a human being has been born into the world" (John 16:21). Can you imagine, even for a moment, that Jesus would refer to childbirth in this joyful way if there were even the faintest chance that a newborn babe had already been marked out for eternal doom? Yet there is no doubt whatsoever that this is what Calvin would have us believe.

For Calvinists to call such a scenario a mystery in any sense of the word is illogical. The mystery is how this grotesque notion could catch on. So let us look at where such a distortion of truth began, since the majority of early church fathers did not think this way.

In speaking of the little children gathered about him, Jesus said, "Even so it is not the will of your Father who is in heaven that one of these little ones should perish" (Matt 18:14). This was also Jesus' desire. So did none of them go to hell? Were they all, without exception, "predestined to salvation"? If, as Calvinism says, God's will is always done on earth, then it is impossible anyway that any of these little ones ever perish. But is this what Jesus really meant?

It was principally Augustine of Hippo, sometimes referred to as the "Father of Roman Catholicism," who introduced these ideas. Is this the kind of Father in heaven that you picture; one who leaves innumerable people to suffer the eternal consequences of their inevitable sin nature without moving a finger? Can you picture Jesus behaving this way with anybody; He who welcomed all the little children around him and rebuked the disciples for any thought of discrimination? "Then little children were brought to Him that He might put His hands on them and pray, but the disciples rebuked them. But Jesus said, 'Let the little children come to Me, and do not forbid them; for of such is the kingdom of heaven'" (Matt 19:13).

I repeat, nowhere does the Bible present predestination as an unexplained "mystery." Moreover, in the only five places in the King James Bible where the word translated "foreordained" or "predestined" occurs (Acts 4:28; 1 Corinthians 2:7; Romans 8:29; and Ephesians 1:5 and 11), being individually saved for heaven, or condemned to hell, are not even mentioned!

Predestination is not about who is destined to become a Christian, but whom a Christian is destined to become.

"For whom He foreknew, He also predestined to be conformed to the image of His Son, that He might be the firstborn among many brethren. Moreover whom He predestined, these He also called; whom He called, these He also justified; and whom He justified, these He also glorified" (Rom 8:29). This text, while referring collectively to the multitude that would believe on His Name, does not single them out as individuals who have, or have not, believed and inherited the blessings. God simply planned that believers would become Jesus' brothers by adoption, and grow more and more like Him. To show that he did not always consistently follow Augustine's distortion of predestination's true meaning, here is part of Calvin's commentary on Romans 8:29:

> The verb proorizo, which some translate, to *predestinate*, is to be understood according to what this passage requires; for Paul only meant, that God had so determined that all whom he has adopted should bear the image of Christ; nor has he simply said, that they were to be conformed to Christ, but to *the image of Christ*, that he might teach us that there is in Christ a living and conspicuous exemplar, which is exhibited to God's children for imitation. The meaning then is, that gratuitous adoption, in which our salvation consists, is inseparable from the other decree, which determines that we are to bear the cross; for no one can be an heir of heaven without being conformed to the image of the only-begotten Son of God.[2]

We notice here that, concerning predestination, Calvin himself, in contrast with his statements elsewhere, placed the emphasis where it rightfully belongs, upon the nature and quality of the Christian life and not upon the initial step into that life.

"Just as He chose us in Him before the foundation of the world, that we should be holy and without blame before Him in love, having predestined us to adoption as sons by Jesus Christ to Himself, according to the good pleasure of His will, to the praise of the glory of His grace, by which He made us accepted in the Beloved" (Eph 1:4–6). These verses do not say He has chosen "some of us" to be saved before the foundation of the world, but that from the foundation of the world His choice is that salvation be in and through Jesus, destining for us a life of practical love and holiness. The emphasis is above all on the quality of that relationship, and on our living holy lives as adopted children, not being mere slaves, in His

2. Calvin, *Romans*, 228.

family. "In Christ also we have obtained an inheritance, being predestined according to the purpose of Him who works all things after the counsel of His own will, that we, who first trusted in Christ, should be to the praise of His glory" (Eph 1:11–12).

Since God is not willing that any should perish, the "all things" here include God's sovereign resolve to preserve human choice and individual responsibility for known sin. To whom does Paul refer here? Note the significant wording: not "we whom God selected to be His children," but "we who first trusted in Christ." These passages refer to the fact that God, in eternity past, established the means by which this wonderful inheritance would come. It would come through Jesus Christ, and all those who choose to believe in Him would become, by His grace, brothers of Jesus, adopted children as distinct from slaves. From now on, we are to live to the praise of His glory, instead of for self, and to grow more like Him day by day. In these passages of Scripture there is not meant to be any suggestion that God arbitrarily chose in advance those whom He will save.

Most Calvinists maintain that "adopted" and "being saved" are the same thing, but this is not so. In Paul's time, if one were enslaved, one might be set free (saved) by some government clemency. One would then no longer belong to anybody, and might again be enslaved at some future date. Or, a kindly person might pay a ransom so that a slave would be set free. He would then be free, but not necessarily adopted into that person's family. Again, a benefactor might set a slave free and make him not just a servant, but also a full member of his own family, in which case he would have been both delivered and adopted. God did not predestine our own particular, individual redemption, but He did sovereignly decide that if we receive His offer of mercy, He would not only save us from our sins, but also go all the way and actually adopt us into His own family. What completeness there is in this wonderful fact of our risen life in Christ! Romans 8:15 also reminds us that we have not received a spirit that makes us slaves, but fully adopted sons of the King of Kings!

Let us note that this wonderful adoption is placed in the future in Romans 8:23: "And not only they, but ourselves also, who have the first-fruits of the Spirit, even we ourselves groan within ourselves, waiting for the adoption, to wit, the redemption of our body." We can enjoy the assured benefits of being delivered from the power of sin here and now, but the full experience of our adoption inheritance awaits the resurrection of our glorified body, when the very presence of sin will be forever banished.

Here is further proof that our being saved and our being adopted are not the same thing.

The spirit of predestination is exemplified in 1 John 3:1a: "Behold what manner of love the Father has bestowed upon us, that we should be called children of God!" We are heirs of the kingdom because we have become His children, not merely His slaves. "And if children, then heirs—heirs of God and joint heirs with Christ, if indeed we suffer with Him, that we may also be glorified together" (Rom 8:17). God wants us to be full members of His family, and inheritors of all of Christ's riches in glory. "Therefore you are no longer a slave but a son, and if a son, then an heir of God through Christ" (Gal 4:7).

Predestination refers to the goal, the destination that God fixed in eternity past for believers in Him.

Consequently, our predestined goal is not about God's work of saving us, but about our becoming brothers and sisters of Jesus, being transformed into His likeness and living for His glory. Whereas predestination is not speaking about which specific individuals God will choose to save, one of its purposes is to comfort believers with the knowledge that the Lord firmly established for us the goal of Christlikeness. He who is the author of our faith is also the finisher (Hebrews 12:2) or "perfecter" of it. However spiritually deficient we feel today, one day we shall truly be like Him, when we see Him face to face: "Beloved, now we are children of God, and it has not yet been revealed what we shall be: but we know that when He is revealed, we shall be like Him, for we shall see Him as He is" (1 John 3:2). God fixed, right from the beginning, the nature, quality, and destiny of the authentic Christian life.

The secret is out! There can no longer be any doubt! We are all invited to become part of God's very own household, not as mere servants, but as brothers and sisters of Jesus, all bearing the family likeness. Other facets of redemption might still be hidden from our eyes, but the central, solid foundation on which we can help to build each other up, is this unmistakable fact that we can all become attractively holy, in and through Christ's redemptive work on our behalf.

Now we can read the following verses again in the light of their true meaning and emphasis: "Just as He chose us in Him before the creation of the world, that we should be holy and without blame before Him in love, having predestined us to adoption as sons by Jesus Christ to Himself, according to the good pleasure of His will" (Eph 1:4–5), and "For whom He foreknew He also predestined to be conformed to the likeness of His Son, that He might be the firstborn among many brethren" (Rom 8:29). Predestination is not about who is destined to become a Christian, but whom a Christian is destined to become.

3

Is the Gospel Good News for All or Is It Bad News for Some?

A TELEVISION INTERVIEWER ONCE asked Billy Graham's daughter, Anne Graham Lotz, the following question: "Is Jesus exclusively the only way to heaven? You know how mad that makes people these days." She replied, "Jesus is not exclusive. He died so that everyone could come to Him for salvation." The word *gospel* means good news. It's not just "news," it is "good news." We can consult daily news bulletins on the Internet, with their mixture of good and bad news, and then select certain people and situations to lift up to God in prayer. We can choose to pay scant attention to the multitude of irrelevancies. The majority of people, however, seem to want to feed upon the crimes, catastrophes, and injustices of this world, and this focus on the negative has, to some extent, conditioned us all. In contrast, however, the gospel itself really is very good news for *everyone*.

In Luke 2:10 the angel announced, "Behold, I bring you *good tidings* of great joy, which will be to all people" (italics mine). Yet the gospel would be very bad news to most people if, in fact, God had made a divine choice before their birth, to consign millions to hell, thus depriving them of any possibility of being redeemed. The Bible describes Jesus as "the Savior of the world," and not just "the Savior of the elect." We must pay careful attention to the occurrences and uses of the words "world" and "all" in Scripture, making sure that we allow the context to guide us as to their meaning and scope. Let us note the use of these two words in the following verses: ". . . because we trust in the living God, *who is the Savior of all men*, especially of those that believe" (1 Tim 4:10; italics mine). Similarly, we need to notice the choice of wording in 1 John 2:2: "And He Himself is the propitiation for our sins, and not for ours only but also *for the whole world*" (italics mine). Is it not urgent that we dispel the dark clouds of misunderstanding and proclaim afresh the truth that the gospel is wonderful news for the entire world, not just for a selected group? Our heavenly Father longs to reveal His redemptive plan to all, including the educationally deprived. The verses quoted above are just two of a number of texts that many Calvinists would love the apostles to have worded differently. Fortunately, their integrity and their deep love and respect for Scripture as the inspired Word of God restrains them from yielding to any desire to misquote the text! In 1 John 2:2, the apostle could have said: ". . . but also for people in every land, or every race, or every kind of person." But he did not say this!

Surely, we should not need special theological training in order to understand the following very plain statements of God's Word, in which Jesus clearly explains why the Father sent Him into the world: "For God did not send His Son *into the world* to condemn the world, but that the world through Him might be saved" (John 3:17; italics mine). Nor should it be difficult to grasp the import of the following: "Now we believe, not because of what you said, for we ourselves have heard Him and we know that this is indeed the Christ, *the Savior of the world*" (John 4:42; italics mine). These verses are explicit and inescapably clear. How can "the world" mean anything else but all human beings? There is an abundance of Greek words that could have been used, applying this propitiation to just "the elect," "the predestined," etc. Fortunately for us, the whole of humankind is stated as the object of His atoning work. For what other reason would the apostles all call Jesus *the Savior of the world,* a term frequently used in the New Testament? "And we have seen and testify that the Father sent the Son as Savior of the world" (1 John 4:14). Jesus, Savior of the world, offers life to all who will choose to receive Him. "For the bread of God is He who comes down from heaven, and gives life to the world" (John 6:33). If He came to give life only unto the world of the elect, would He not have said so?

Who are the "whosoever" in John 3:16: ". . . that whosoever believes in Him should not perish, but have everlasting life"? In addition, what is the "world" in the next verse? "God did not send His Son into the world to condemn the world, but that the world through Him might be saved" (John 3:17). We can ask ourselves why, where Paul is speaking to the Jews in Romans 11:15, he uses the following terminology: "For if their being cast away is the reconciling of the world, what will their acceptance be but life from the dead?" Do you think Paul was referring to just the elect, or to the whole world?

Taken from his commentary on the gospel of John, this is what Calvin had to say about John 3:16:

> The Heavenly Father loves the human race and wishes that they should not perish. He has employed the universal term "whoever" both to invite all indiscriminately to partake of life and to cut off every excuse of unbelievers. He shows himself to be reconciled to the whole world when He invites all men without exception to the faith of Christ.[1]

Exactly! Well said, Calvin! What could be more plain? Yet, sadly, in the very next paragraph, he limits its extent by saying that only the elect have faith bestowed upon them to enable them to trust in Christ! Again, in his commentary on 1 Timothy 2:4, he says that God has at heart the salvation of all, and his comment on 2 Peter 3:9 is that He invites all to the acknowledgement of His truth. Then, in both instances, Calvin proceeds again to limit the "all" by saying that it really only means "all kinds," although both Paul and Peter could have said "all kinds" if that was what they meant. There are Hebrew and Greek words that convey the sense of "all kinds," such as those exemplified in Matthew 5:11: "Blessed are you when . . . they say all kinds of evil against you." (See also Ecclesiastes 2:5; Ephesians 6:18; Matthew 13:47; Luke 12:15; Acts 2:39, 10:12; 1 Timothy 5:10; James 3:7; 1 Peter 1:6; and Hebrews 13:9.)

It is surely well worthwhile to quote another of Calvin's intriguing comments:

> ". . . *who wishes that all men may be saved*" (1Tim 2:4). Here follows a confirmation of the second argument; and what is more reasonable than that all our prayers should be in conformity with this decree of God? "*And may come to the acknowledgment of the truth.*" Lastly, he [Paul] demonstrates that God has at heart the salvation of all, because He invites all to the acknowledgment of His truth. This belongs to that kind of argument in which the cause is proved from the effect for, if "the gospel is the power of God for salvation to every one that believeth" (Rom 1:16), it is certain that all those to whom the gospel is addressed are invited to the hope of eternal life. In short, as the calling is a proof of the secret election, so they whom God makes partakers of His gospel are

---

1. Calvin, *Gospel of John*, 123–25.

admitted by Him to possess salvation; because the gospel reveals to us the righteousness of God, which is a sure entrance into life. Hence we see the childish folly of those who represent this passage to be opposed to predestination. "If God" say they, "wishes all men indiscriminately to be saved, it is false that some are predestined by His eternal purpose to salvation, and others to perdition." They might have had some ground for saying this, if Paul were speaking here about individual men; although even then we should not have wanted the means of replying to their argument; for, although the will of God ought not to be judged from His secret decrees, when He reveals them to us by outward signs, yet it does not therefore follow that He has not determined with Himself what He intends to do as to every individual man. But I say nothing on that subject, because it has nothing to do with this passage; for the Apostle simply means, that there is no people and no rank in the world that is excluded from salvation; because God wishes that the gospel should be proclaimed to all without exception. Now the preaching of the gospel gives life; and hence he justly concludes that God invites all equally to partake of salvation. But the present discourse relates to classes of men, and not to individual persons; for his sole object is, to include in this number princes and foreign nations. That God wishes the doctrine of salvation to be enjoyed by them as well as others, is evident from the passages already quoted, and from other passages of a similar nature.[2]

If our commitment to Jesus is altogether practical, and we are seeking with all our heart to accomplish His will in our everyday life, then God promises to communicate the true doctrines of His grace to us. Let us not be merely intellectual about this important issue. Spiritual matters are mainly things of the heart and spirit, and not primarily of the mind, and we must be willing to open our heart to receive the plain statements of Scripture by faith. This truth is again exemplified by Paul when he says, "But God be thanked, that though you were the servants of sin, yet you obeyed *from the heart* that form of doctrine to which you were delivered" (Rom 6:17).

"If anyone wants to do His will, he shall know concerning the doctrine, whether it is from God or whether I speak on My own authority" (John 7:17). Let our consideration of this important issue be more than just intellectual or cerebral. Are we allowing the plain statements of Scripture to speak directly to our heart—to our inmost being—which is

2. Calvin, *2 Timothy*, 54–55.

the seat of our will? For some people, grasping various aspects of God's sovereignty, or His plan of salvation, may indeed primarily only involve their intellect, whereas love is supremely a matter of the heart. Full appreciation of the great love of God our Father comes through developing our heart-relationship with Him. In Exodus 28:15–30, we read about Aaron's breastplate: "You shall make the breastplate of judgment . . ." (v.15). "So Aaron shall bear the names of the sons of Israel on the breastplate of judgment (of decision, NIV) over his heart when he goes into the holy place" (v.29). "And you shall put in the breastplate of judgment the Urim and Thummin, and they shall be upon Aaron's heart when he goes in before the Lord: and so Aaron shall bear the judgment of the children of Israel over his heart before the Lord continually" (v.30).

If decisions were primarily a matter of the mind, then would not the Lord have had the Urim and Thummin placed on the helmet rather than on the breastplate? In Ephesians 6:14, Paul refers to righteousness as a breastplate, signifying again that our will, attitudes, and obedience, or "doctrine" in the New Testament sense, have their source in our heart and not in our head.

The following verses, which are just a few among dozens found in the Word of God, also make it plain that the center of our being and the seat of our will and disposition is in our heart, our inmost being, as distinct from being in our head. Let us notice first of all the contrast between trusting in our own understanding of an issue, and leaning upon the Lord with our whole heart: "Trust in the Lord with all your heart and lean not on your own understanding" (Prov 3:5). We can never be in actual possession of all the facts concerning a person or situation, simply because the Lord alone reserves for Himself the ability to discern the hidden motives of people's hearts. As the overwhelming significance of knowing more of the true condition of our own heart dawns upon us, we can then start changing gears, and giving the dispositions of our inner life earnest attention before the Lord. "Keep your heart with all diligence; for out of it spring the issues of life" (Prov 4:23). Life's grand options, and also its hidden danger areas, can be in great measure correctly discerned and appropriate action taken, provided that we learn to tremble at any lack of vigilance on our part concerning the keeping of our own heart. Job expressed this most significant dimension of the heart when he said, "At this also my heart trembles, and leaps from its place" (Job 37:1). It is the Lord's settled desire for His people that genuine truthfulness and resulting wisdom rule in our inmost being. "Behold, You desire truth in the inward parts, and in the hidden part You will make me to know wisdom" (Ps 51:6).

"From the heart" is a recurrent phrase in the Bible, as in Isaiah 59:13, "...conceiving and uttering from the heart words of falsehood." To modern ears, "from the heart" may not seem significant. However, no words of Scripture can be treated as incidental or redundant. In the Bible, the Holy Spirit often mentions different parts of our makeup, frequently drawing attention to what is going on in the depths of our inner life. In order to be transformed into Christ's likeness, we need to be constantly in touch with our inmost being. None of us can afford, at any time, to allow our intellect alone to be cultivated while neglecting our heart life, nor dare we neglect cultivation of a spiritual mind, as it needs to be trained and controlled. There is further proof of this where, in Romans 12:1, Paul exhorts us to offer *our body* to God in order that our mind be renewed. For instance, regularly offering, in specific detail, all of our private body parts to God can become the best of all protections against committing sexual sin. This principle equally applies to our eyes. Offering our eyes to Jesus each day will help us look upon only those things that are profitable and build us up. Offering our ears to God will help us to fulfill the encouragement found in James 1:19, where each of us are told rather to be slow to speak and quick to listen. Above all, as James also reminds us, our mouths need to be brought under His dominion. Let us offer our tongue to the Lord each day, that we might say only helpful things to others, and become a source of encouragement, rather than of criticism and complaint.

Let us return to TULIP—the five main points of Calvin's theological system—according to which the Holy Spirit must regenerate a person before he can believe and put his trust in Christ! Consider Peter's analysis of what is happening in Cornelius's household in Acts 10:34–48, because much of what happened hardly seems to fit the five points of Calvinism mentioned in our Introduction. Peter asserts that:

1. God does not show any kind of favoritism (Acts 10:34).

2. Cornelius is living an exemplary life of genuine piety even before receiving the gift of the Holy Spirit (Acts 10:30–31).

3. Jesus Christ is said to be the "Lord of all," and not just Lord of a selected group (Acts 10:35, 43; 11:18).

4. Cornelius, his family, and his close friends receive the Holy Spirit before being baptized in water. Also note that they put their trust in the Lord, and God then gives them His Holy Spirit (Acts 10:44–48).

5. God grants repentance to the Gentiles and not just to the Jews (Acts 11:18).

As we have said, Calvin maintained that God chooses to withhold from many people the indispensable grace they need in order to turn to Him in repentance and faith. This would indeed be very bad news for most people. It would mean that unless God sovereignly chooses to intervene, a criminal would be left *inevitably* to commit more atrocities, such as maiming, killing, and creating more victims, with all the attendant misery and despair. Frankly, who in the world would want a God like that? We are left wondering what purpose there is in trying to deny the fact of human freedom of choice implied throughout the pages of Scripture. Is it because avoiding it makes fewer demands on us? What are we supposed to make of the following clear statement of God's will: "For this is good and acceptable in the sight of God our Savior, *who desires all men to be saved* and to come to the knowledge of the truth. For there is one God and one Mediator between God and men, the Man Christ Jesus, who gave Himself a ransom for all, to be testified in due time" (1 Tim 2:3; italics mine). Further along in this letter, Paul reminds Timothy that ". . . to this end we both labor and suffer reproach, because we trust in the living God, who is the Savior of all men, especially of those who believe" (1 Tim 4:10).

Our hearts need to be filled daily with the love of God, flooding our affections, captivating our soul, enabling us to worship Him all day in spirit and truth. Even correct religious opinions and orthodox theology, if limited to our human understanding, cannot produce genuine spiritual fruit. We can zealously defend our opinions and have correct views on major doctrines, yet remain unfamiliar with true religion of the heart. Above all, let us cling tenaciously to the glorious truth that the gospel expresses God's unconditional love to all mankind, and that no thought of excluding anybody was ever in His heart. It is certainly true that many are ultimately excluded, but this is because they have chosen to exclude themselves, not that God had any secret intent to doom them.

4

Does God Want to Save Only the Elect?

IMAGINE THIS SCENARIO: TWO lads are wading in a river when suddenly the swift current grabs them and they risk drowning. A man out walking his dog sees the lads floundering in the turbulent water and grabs one of the life preservers hanging on a wooden cross on the bank. He throws a life preserver to one boy but does not attempt to help the other, even though there are two life preservers and he has the ability and strength to do so. What callous behavior that would be! In many countries, it is a crime not to do what one reasonably can to assist someone in mortal danger.

Using that analogy, is it not slanderous to maintain that God, who is Love, would place the life preserver of salvation within reach of one but not the other, when both are equally in desperate need of rescue and help, and both have the strength to grab one? Would He not throw out both life preservers, longing to see both lads respond by reaching out and seizing them? Even our own finite sense of compassion should help us to identify the just and righteous acts that are motivated by compassion. We can indeed expect to discern justice and righteousness in the spirit of Proverbs 28:5: "Evil men do not understand justice, but those who seek the Lord understand all." Even Augustine of Hippo said that the idea was abhorrent that God picks and chooses only certain persons for salvation, for reasons known only to Him. How tragic that such repugnant ideas did not lead him to investigate more deeply the true significance of predestination, and to discover that God never violates man's freedom by forcing him to follow Him.

God's holy righteousness and justice need never be at variance with a spiritual man's concept of righteousness and justice; otherwise, what would it mean to be created in God's image and restored to fellowship with Him? True conversion to Christ heightens our sense of justice. Are we then to believe that God would act in violation of our highest sense of holy justice? Never! If it depended upon God alone to decide whom He would save, we can be sure that He would save everybody (See 1 Timothy 2: 3–4 and 2 Peter 3:9).

Jesus Himself clearly states the reason for His coming into the world when He says, "I have come as a light into the world, that whoever believes in Me should not abide in darkness. And if anyone hears My words and does not believe, I do not judge him; for I did not come to judge the world but to save the world" (John 12:46–47). And, without question, God states in Ezekiel that the death of the wicked brings Him no pleasure at all, so it follows that selectively and arbitrarily withholding grace from anyone would also bring Him no pleasure or glory. To reinforce this fact, He repeats this truth: "'Do I have any pleasure at all that the wicked should die,' says the Lord God, 'and not that he should turn from his ways and live?'" (Ezek 18:23). He continues, "Say to them: 'As I live,' says the Lord God, 'I have no pleasure in the death of the wicked, but that the wicked turn from his way and live. Turn, turn from your evil ways! For why should you die, O house of Israel?'" (Ezek 33:11).

In spite of this, some Christians believe that God does act arbitrarily towards sinners, choosing to help some but not others. However, in Acts 10:34 (NIV) we read that "God does not show favoritism." God does not capriciously pick out favorites! What a blessing it is for us that He is full of impartial justice, and infinitely more compassionate than we are.

Let me emphasize that there is no suggestion here of universalism, the belief that all who have ever lived on earth will be welcomed into heaven. For us to "always be with the Lord" (1 Thess 4:17) after this life, we need to seek, repent, believe, and receive the Lord into our heart, and pursue a new goal: to live a life of holiness.

Calvinists teach that if we were to exercise our own authentic freedom of choice as we accept God's offer of salvation, it would constitute some kind of merit on our part and detract from God's sovereignty. However, earthly authorities sometimes offer a pardon to convicted criminals, and prisoners would be most unlikely to refuse it. Does gladly receiving the pardon make the prisoner meritorious? Surely, it merely magnifies the kindness of the one who offers the pardon! What merit or special ability of any kind do we need to receive a gift? Do we praise people for accepting a present? Of course not! Normally the giver gets the thanks and praise.

As already stated, some maintain that our individual salvation is solely dependent upon an elective choice on God's part. If we deny the "whosoever will may come" that ends Philip Bliss's familiar hymn, "Whosoever
heareth, shout, shout the sound," are we not then like puppets, mere
marionettes, with our responses entirely dependent on how God pulls the
strings? Furthermore, where we read in Romans 11:28, referring to the
Jews, "Concerning the gospel they are enemies for your sake, but concerning the election they are beloved for the sake of the fathers," we must ask
how God's chosen people could be, at the same time, both enemies of the
gospel and yet beloved concerning the election? "Election" here cannot
be referring to the matter of salvation as such, but to the function and
role the Jews were meant to fulfill in bringing salvation to the world. In
verse 20 of the same chapter, we are reminded that some of the Jews were
branches broken off because of their unbelief, rather than as a result of a
divine decree or an elective choice on God's part. They simply refused to
seek God's wisdom and to trust in His Word. Instead of conscientiously
following their father Abraham's example, they chose to cling to the works
of the Law, and even added to them, in order to gain favor with God.

The Bible never refers to election as something hidden from our
understanding. It speaks of election as a "purpose." So what is that purpose? Referring to Jacob and Esau, Paul states, "For the children not yet
being born, nor having done any good or evil, that the purpose of God
according to election might stand, not of works, but of Him who calls,
it was said to her, 'the older shall serve the younger'" (Rom 9:11–12). It
ought to be obvious that this reference is not talking about salvation at
all, but of "serving." The Lord chose the earthly role that these two nations
would fulfill (see Romans 9:11). Then, in verse 12, we read about God
loving Jacob and hating Esau, and that the older would serve the younger.
However, Esau, as an individual, never did serve Jacob!

In Malachi 1:2–3, we read: "I have loved you," says the Lord. "Yet you
say, 'In what way have You loved us?' Was not Esau Jacob's brother?" says
the Lord. "Yet Jacob [Israel] I have loved, but Esau [Edom] I have hated,
and laid waste his mountains and his heritage for the jackals of the wilderness." Clearly, the text is not speaking of these two individuals but is
referring to the respective roles of the race that descended from each,
Israel and Edom; and to the consequences, in God's unfolding plan of
redemption, of their heart attitudes to Him.

In addition, when it says "hated" regarding Esau, we should see this as being similar to Jesus' use of the word in His statement about hating our father and mother in Luke 14:26. God did not use the word "hate" in the way we use it, but implied a lesser love, employing a term of comparison in keeping with language usage in that culture. God chose to make Jacob and his descendents the object of His special love and attention, revealing Himself to the world through Jacob, which is the nation of Israel, rather than through Esau, the nation of Edom.

Further, God clearly instructed the Israelites not to hate the Edomites: "You shall not abhor an Edomite, for he is your brother: you shall not abhor an Egyptian, because you were an alien in his land" (Deut 23:7). So would God have told the Israelites not to abhor a race that He Himself actually hated, in our meaning of the word today?

In Romans 1:16 Paul reminds us that salvation is for everyone who believes, and not just for the "elect": "For I am not ashamed of the gospel of Christ, for it is the power of God to salvation for everyone who believes, for the Jew first and also for the Greek" (Rom 1:16). Significantly, Paul writes to Timothy about his suffering for the gospel in these terms: "Therefore I endure all things for the sake of the elect, that they also may obtain the salvation which is in Christ Jesus with eternal glory" (2 Tim 2:10). If God saves the "elect" uniquely by divine decree, how could Paul's enduring anything at all for their sake contribute to their obtaining salvation? Furthermore, to be consistent, the TULIP theological system's premise would demand that one ask what could be the actual purpose of prevailing intercession for the lost. Those marked out for eternal death by God would not get their destiny altered by our intercession, nor would our prayers help toward the salvation of others, since their salvation would depend solely upon God's prior decision to that effect. Certainly intercession in the Holy Spirit is a mysterious but very real privilege, and prayer does indeed change things in the objective realm and not just in the subjective.

If our individual salvation were to depend exclusively upon God's elective choice, why then does the Bible refer to Israel as God's elect nation? "For Jacob My servant's sake, and Israel My elect, I have even called you by your name" (Isa 45:4). Does calling Israel "My elect" mean that God saves all the Jews regardless of their chosen attitude towards Him? Again we say, of course not!

We do not need to give the word "election" in the Bible a different meaning to that in current English. We elect representatives from among those freely willing to stand, and then once elected these people can be chosen for some specific office or role.

What is the spiritual purpose of election? There are two aspects to the principle of election. One concerns vocational function and type of ministry. Election often refers to God's sovereign choice regarding His methods in the unfolding plan of redemption, communicating to us which role He will assign to which person. The other aspect refers to all the spiritual privileges we enjoy as part of our inheritance in Christ. Abraham is a fine example of the former aspect of election. His election does not mean that he was the only honorable man on earth, or the only person God sought to save at that time. Look at the upright manner in which even Gentiles like Abimelech dealt with both Abraham and Isaac in Genesis 20 and 26. Jethro, the Midianite priest and father-in-law of Moses, was another example of those who, though not in Abraham's lineage, honored and served God (see Genesis 14:18 and Exodus 18:10). God was not only interested in eternally saving Abraham, but His plan was also to reveal Himself to all humanity through His dealings with a chosen group of people: Abraham's descendants through Isaac.

Election also describes God's less obvious choices of people whom He will use to accomplish His plans, for in His elective purposes, God sometimes passes over the firstborn in the granting of earthly privileges, as in the following episode.

> Now when Joseph saw that his father laid his right hand on the head of Ephraim, it displeased him; so he took hold of his father's hand to remove it from Ephraim's head to Manasseh's head. And Joseph said to his father, "Not so, my father, for this one is the firstborn; put your right hand on his head." But his father refused and said, "I know, my son, I know. He also shall become a people, and he also shall be great; but truly his younger brother shall be greater than he, and his descendants shall become a multitude of nations." So he blessed them that day, saying, "By you Israel will bless, saying, 'May God make you as Ephraim and as Manasseh!'" And thus he set Ephraim before Manasseh. (Gen 48:17–20)

Jesus is the "Elect" of God, and we who are in Him share in this election and in the fulfillment of God's purpose for our life. "Behold my servant, whom I uphold, my Elect One in whom My soul delights! I have put My Spirit upon Him; He will bring forth justice to the Gentiles" (Isa 42:1). Here the word "elect" refers to the special role given to Jesus in the plan of redemption, and obviously not to the salvation of Jesus! The New Testament elect are those who function "in Christ." "Election" encompasses all that we inherit as members of His body, the church. Our salvation is not just an escape from hell, but also a rich inheritance, a whole quality of life finding its full expression in the new heavens and earth, when with our resurrected bodies, we will be free from the limitations of this present order of things.

Are "calling" and "election" therefore immutable decrees, whose outworking in human life are unaffected by man's responses and choices? Peter does not seem to think so: "Therefore, brethren, be even more diligent to make your call and election sure: for if you do these things you will never stumble" (2 Pet 1:10). The context of this verse encourages us to pursue those qualities that are essential for a fruitful Christian life, reminding us again that our calling and election are to a special quality of life and service, fulfilling the good works God prepared for us individually. He encourages us to go on striving to enter our full inheritance—another indication that we do not possess it all automatically by divine decree.

Are there times when God's election annuls man's freedom of choice? For instance, did God override Saul's will on the Damascus road? It is significant how the Lord dialogues with Saul: "Then he fell to the ground, and heard a voice saying to him, 'Saul, Saul, why are you persecuting Me?' And he said, 'Who are You, Lord?' Then the Lord said, 'I am Jesus, whom you are persecuting. It is hard for you to kick against the goads.' So he, trembling and astonished, said, 'Lord, what do You want me to do?' Then the Lord said to him, 'Arise and go into the city, and you will be told what you must do'" (Acts 9:4–6).

Did this spectacular divine intervention, when Jesus so dramatically intervened in his life, disable Saul's own will to the point that he was unable to refuse God's call? Nothing in this passage intends to convey this. Saul had instigated cruel persecution of Christians, then had witnessed Stephen's glorious testimony while being stoned, and certainly was subsequently trying to ignore the pricks of his prejudice-crammed conscience. We can imagine the battle that had been raging in his spirit; his pharisaic upbringing and training tugging him one way, and what he had recently witnessed pulling him in a different, unknown, and uncharted direction.

How many people have been spoken to very clearly by God but have subsequently refused to follow Him! All that some folk have needed, in order to respond positively, was a sweet and gentle whisper from the Lord, whereas with others He has had to "shout" through much suffering. We do not know what transpires in people's hearts. God's wonderful ways in reaching people are beyond our understanding. An intriguing example of this principle is found in John 4:38, where Jesus tells his twelve disciples that He had sent them out to reap where others had labored. They had merely joined in the work of people whose identity and ministry are not described here in any detail. We usually associate the organized evangelism of Jesus' time with the activities of the twelve, or the seventy, mentioned in Luke 10:1. Here is an example, within Scripture, of God at work on a much vaster scale than is recorded. Who were those who had tilled the soil, sown it, and watered it in order that His small circle of helpers might go reaping? We can be sure that at no time does He act purely arbitrarily, or in a coercive manner, in His dealings with those who seek Him.

Does the following passage in Romans 11:2–5 suggest a sovereign act of God, as some would have it, without any reference to the prophets' free choices?

> God has not cast away His people whom He foreknew. Or do you not know what the Scripture says of Elijah, how he pleads with God against Israel, saying, "Lord, they have killed Your prophets and torn down Your altars, and I alone am left, and they seek my life"? But what does the divine response say to him? "I have reserved for Myself seven thousand men who have not bowed the knee to Baal." Even so then, at this present time there is a remnant according to the election of grace.

This passage does not infer that it was God who had stopped these seven thousand Israelites from bowing the knee to Baal. These men had chosen obedience to God, with His help, and so God had set them aside and reserved them for Himself. Besides, this whole section in Romans is bringing out the contrast between the spirit of grace and that of works, not alluding to the question of God's sovereignty and man's full responsibility. Today, those who appropriate God's grace, renouncing any thought of counting on their own works in order to earn anything from God, are elected to be participators in the work of the Lord Jesus Christ, as part of the body of which He is the head.

To sum up regarding election, the New Testament emphasis is upon the nature and quality of all that we, as believers, possess in Jesus, rather than on God having arbitrarily selected those persons who would benefit from such blessings. The principle of election stands grounded in God's sovereign will, without in any measure violating man's freedom of choice.

> *We are numbered among the elect because*
> *we have become part of the body of Christ,*
> *rather than part of Christ's body because*
> *we were among those elected to salvation.*

Several citations from the Old Testament remind us again of God's earnest desire to bless, but men's unwillingness to trust Him: "If you are willing and obedient, you shall eat the good of the land; but if you refuse and rebel, you shall be devoured by the sword" (Isa 1:19–20). God was willing, but would they be willing? Many Israelites sank to rejecting scornfully the way of wisdom: "Because you disdained all my counsel, and would have none of my rebuke, I also will laugh at your calamity" (Prov 1:25, 30). "But My people would not heed My voice, And Israel would have none of Me" (Ps 81:11). God longed to bless them, but they consistently refused to pay the price of obedience. His own chosen people closed their ears to His voice: "To whom He said, 'This is the rest with which You may cause the weary to rest,' and, 'this is the refreshing'; yet they would not hear" (Isa 28:12). Yet God's invitations were so wholesome, so full of potential blessings: "For thus says the Lord God, the Holy One of Israel: In returning and rest you shall be saved; in quietness and confidence shall be your strength. But you would not" (Isa 30:15). The rebels simply refused God's most gracious offers of rest; that same rest that Jesus calls us all to find in Him—the rest our souls so badly need.

Here is the clearest statement of God's intent, found at the birth of the church in Acts 3:26: "To you first, God, having raised up His Servant Jesus, sent Him to bless you, in turning away every one of you from his iniquities." Our heavenly Father's desire to turn "every one" away from sin is patently obvious, the only impediment being our continued refusal to trust in Him. This "every one" encompassed even those who had caused Christ to be crucified: "Repent therefore and be converted, that your sins

33

may be blotted out, so that times of refreshing may come from the presence of the Lord" (Acts 3:19).

5

Who Are the Called?

WHEN SCHOLARS WORK ON translating the Bible, they try to choose contemporary, everyday words that best convey the meaning of the original language. Although living languages like English grow steadily and change, the word "calling" in English still refers to what we do as distinct from who we are. "Calling" refers to our function in life. Some of us are tall and some short, others are as thin as a beanpole, but we do not refer to these as "callings." In contrast, medical work, architecture, engineering, or inventing would all be callings or vocations. Within the Body of Christ, there are numerous callings, including prophetic ministry, teaching, miracle working, healing, practical help, and administrations. (See 1 Corinthians 12:28.) Calling primarily describes our occupation and service. The apostle Paul was forever mindful of the function that God assigned to him: "Paul, called to be an apostle of Jesus Christ through the will of God" (1 Cor 1:1).

In Peter's second epistle, there is an important verse that further helps us to understand calling. As we work out God's plan for us, we are to examine ourselves and ensure that we are fulfilling God's elective call on the life that now belongs to Him: "Therefore brethren, be even more diligent to make your calling and election sure, for if you do these things you will never stumble" (2 Pet 1:10). There is no suggestion here that calling and election are independent of human freedom of choice, and Peter tells us to be more diligent in working them out. Peter is reminding us that we have to learn to exercise discipline and perseverance in our commitment, so that God might fulfill all His good plans in us.

How are we to understand the meaning of *called* in Romans 8:30: "Moreover, whom He predestined, these He also called; whom He called, these He also justified; and whom He justified, these He also glorified"? Depending on the context, calling has various shades of meaning in the

Bible, but in relation to predestination it means that when we enter into the inheritance of Jesus, the Called One, He imputes to us His own character qualities and righteousness, so that through His strength we are called to become saints. Because of this calling, He enables us to pursue the goal of a holy lifestyle, developing our character and gifts in effective ministry for His glory. In this regard no genuine Christian is exempt from the call to be built up in His church, as expressed in Ephesians 2:22: "... in whom you also are being built together for a dwelling place of God in the Spirit." Here is how Peter puts it: "You also, as living stones, are being built up a spiritual house, a holy priesthood, to offer up spiritual sacrifices acceptable to God through Jesus Christ" (1 Pet 2:5).

Furthermore, Paul urges us to "walk worthy of the calling with which you are called" (Eph 4:1). Therefore, this calling is not something to which we passively assent, but a compellingly powerful incentive to enter conscientiously into the blessings we inherit in Christ, and become wholehearted in following Him. Nowhere is inevitability implied regarding this growth in Christlikeness in our earthly life, as if our willing cooperation was not essential. Indeed, observing our behavior as Christians confirms that our growth depends on our eager surrender to Christ each day, submitting to Him and obeying Him wholeheartedly. This passion for Jesus needs daily nurturing so that we can become convincing witnesses to a watching world.

In Matthew 22:14 Jesus sums up a parable with the solemn words, "Many are called, but few are chosen." In the context of this parable of the king sending servants to bring guests in to the marriage feast of his son, a better translation would be "invited" rather than "called," as in the NIV translation of the Bible. They are all invited, but few of them are chosen, due to their unwillingness to forsake their own self-righteous ways, and not because the king has somehow unilaterally legislated concerning their status.

What then can we say about the following affirmation: "For the gifts and the calling of God are irrevocable" (Rom 11:29)? Here calling is associated with the destiny God sovereignly imparted to Israel to become the means of His revelation of Himself to mankind. It reminds us of the beautiful balance and symmetry between God's sovereignty and our own autonomous will. Take, for example, 1 Corinthians 7:20: "Let each man remain in the same calling in which he was called." Clearly, this verse, with its underlying inference of human options, is referring to the particular context of a Christian's practical walk in life, like being slave or free, married or single, circumcised or uncircumcised, as distinct from the fact of being saved.

You might wonder what Paul means when he says, "I press toward the goal for the prize of the upward call of God in Christ Jesus" (Phil 3:14). Is this prize Paul's ticket into heaven, or is he referring to the rewards he will receive for faithfully fulfilling his appointed ministry? It is wholly legitimate to take it as meaning rewards for the faithful fulfillment of his assignments as an appointed and anointed apostle. Paul is pressing on to know the Lord in a deeper way, but no inevitability is implied or even hinted at.

Nowhere in Scripture is there a hint that calling and election are independent of human co-operation. However, we read "For the gifts and calling of God are irrevocable." (Rom 11:29). Here calling is associated with the gifts God sovereignly imparts to us for ministry as members of His body, but we must be willing to exercise such gifts. Paul urges us to covet earnestly the best gifts, yet the Holy Spirit is the One who chooses them, reminding us again of the effective balance between God's symmetry and our own will (1 Cor 12:31). By our commitment to Jesus Christ, and by our subsequent actions, we need to demonstrate to the world that we are worthy of our calling. "Therefore we also pray always for you that our God would count you worthy of this calling, and fulfill all the good pleasure of His goodness and the work of faith with power" (2 Thess 1:11).

The following verse does not say that God "called us to be saved," but rather, "Who has saved us and called us with a holy calling, not according to our works, but according to His own purpose and grace which was given to us in Christ Jesus before time began" (2 Tim 1:9). The emphasis is that God's purpose would be accomplished through Jesus, and not through works of the law. His grand redemptive design would be fulfilled through His Son, Who would enable us to become holy in His sight. In fact, nowhere does it say in the Scriptures that we were "called to be saved." The emphasis in calling is on the type and quality of life of ministry that God has established for those who enter into living relationship with Him.

If calling were simply a matter of God saving us, then once accomplished, He would surely stop calling there and then. If you call someone to you and he comes, you do not then continue to call him! Worldly wisdom, prestige, and especially materialism, can become big hindrances to hearing God's call. This is not God's doing, but the result is often a failure to heed God: "For you see your calling, brethren, that not many wise according to the flesh, not many mighty, not many noble, are called" (1 Cor 1:26).

Very interestingly, Paul reminds the Corinthian church that they have been called to be saints, thus emphasizing again not just what we become in His sight when born again, but also the ongoing experience of a holy walk in the Christian life: "To the church of God which is at Corinth, to those who are sanctified in Christ Jesus, called to be saints" (1 Cor 1:2). Again, in the following quote, the focus is on God's glory and future kingdom: "That you would walk worthy of God, who calls you into His own Kingdom and glory" (1 Thess 2:12). We see once more this predominant theme of that special quality of life found in Jesus when the *called* and *calling* occur: "For God did not call us unto uncleanness, but in holiness" (1 Thess 4:7).

We might conclude by stating that calling has more to do with the quality of the Christian life itself, rather than referring to the process whereby God initiates us into it.

6

What Is the Role of the Potter?

ONE TYPICALLY HOT SUMMER's day in Provence, France, I had the most-welcome opportunity to watch a potter at work. His foot paddled away, controlling the speed of the spinning wheel, leaving both hands free for the intricate shaping of a vase. Glazing and then firing it in the precise temperature of the oven would follow. The work of a potter is just one of the many illustrations in Scripture that portray God's relationships with His children. Other relational images include shepherd to sheep (John 10:11), bridegroom to bride (John 3:29), father to sons (Luke 15:21), master to servants (Luke 12:46), friend to friends (John 15:14), king to subjects, (Matthew 18:23), sower to seed (Matthew 13:3), and vine to branches, (John 15:5).

In our search for the truth, we need to compare relevant Bible passages that describe our relationship with God, in order to guard against misinterpreting their meaning. "Does not the potter have power over the clay, from the same lump to make one vessel for honor and another for dishonor" (Rom 9:21)? Let us submit these words of Paul's to that general rule, for this illustration has been much misused by those who apply it in an attempt to buttress Calvin's interpretations. They imply that humans closely resemble *passive* lumps of clay, even though this thought was not in the apostle's mind at all.

In Romans 9:21, the prophet Jeremiah is the chief inspiration for Paul's illustration of the potter and the clay. There it is unmistakable that God is speaking of His dealings with nations, rather than with individuals: "'O house of Israel, can I not do with you as with this potter?' says the Lord. 'Look, as the clay is in the potter's hand, so are you in My hand, O house of Israel. The instant I speak concerning a nation, and concerning a kingdom, to pluck up, to pull down, and to destroy it, if that nation, against whom I have spoken, turn from its evil, *I will relent* of the disaster I thought to bring upon it '" (Jer 18:6–8; italics mine).

Did you notice that there is no predetermination, inevitability, or immutability about this statement? These verses speak pointedly about the Lord refraining from carrying out His punitive measures, or at least reducing them, if there is repentance. It ought to be obvious that the Lord will change His own plan if the respective nation or person turns to Him in repentance, even as He changed plans over the city of Nineveh in Jonah 3:10. However, sinners always have to bear at least some of the temporal consequences of their choices and consequent actions.

In keeping with this imagery, the passage in Romans is *not* suddenly introducing a new concept, nor is it presenting an unchangeable decree. God will form to honor or dishonor the "clay" of which individuals and nations are made, depending on their attitude to Him. Furthermore, the choice in the potter's creations is between noble purposes and common use, rather than salvation or damnation. Here again the Word is speaking of roles as distinct from individual salvation. (Of course, God can and does extend mercy to whomever He pleases, and only He knows when a heart has been hardened beyond redemption.) Remember that God grants salvation through perfect love, not through any obligation or coercion.

As with every other metaphor, we must not press this portrayal of God as a potter too far, because people, with their feelings and desires, are very different from clay, which is inert and has no will of its own. Paul's desire, in picking up Jeremiah's illustration concerning the potter and the clay, is to emphasize God's sovereign response to the free choices of nations and individuals. He uses the same imagery in exhorting Timothy: "But in a great house there are not only vessels of gold and of silver, but also of wood and of earth, some for honor, and some for dishonor. Therefore if anyone *cleanses himself* from the latter, he will be a vessel for honor, sanctified and useful for the Master, prepared for every good work" (2 Tim 2:20–21; italics mine). There is no implication here either of fatality, inevitability, or divine determinism. Let us consistently desist from reading into the text what is not in fact there.

We notice also that Romans 9:22–24 is asking a question rather than making a statement: "What if God, wanting to show His wrath and to make His power known, endured with much longsuffering the vessels of wrath prepared for destruction; and that He might make known the riches of His glory on the vessels of mercy, which He had prepared beforehand for glory, even us whom He has called, not of the Jews only, but also of the Gentiles?" This is similar to my asking you: "What if I invited you to dinner tomorrow night?" It does not mean that I have already invited you, but only that I am considering the idea, and I have not mentioned the facts on which my eventual invitation might be based. Because these verses in Romans chapter 9 form a question and not a statement, it ought to seem obvious that we cannot use them to support any particular doctrinal stance. In any case, this passage does *not* say that it was God who prepared the vessels of wrath for destruction. There are other examples in the book of Jeremiah, and elsewhere in Scripture, of God's desire to relent and not follow through on prophetic utterances, provided that His warnings and threats produce a genuine change of heart among the people. The following passage clearly illustrates this important principle:

> "Perhaps everyone will listen and turn from his evil way, that I may relent concerning the calamity which I purpose to bring on them because of the evil of their doings. And you shall say to them, 'Thus says the Lord: *If you will not listen to Me*, to walk in My law which I have set before you, to heed the words of My servants the prophets whom I sent to you, both rising up early and sending them (but you have not heeded), then I will make this house like Shiloh, and will make this city a curse to all the nations of the earth.'" (Jer 26:3–6; italics mine)

Although many Jews remained under God's wrath because of their persistence in resisting Him, many others did eventually repent, notably at Pentecost, becoming "vessels unto honor." What finer example is there than the apostle Paul, who became an outstanding example of this radical change of heart? In speaking of his fellow countrymen, concerning their difficulty in seeing Christ in the pages of the Old Testament, Paul explains: "Nevertheless, when one turns to the Lord, the veil will be taken away" (2 Cor 3:16); not the other way round. Notice that they must turn to the Lord *before* the veil is removed. God is not the cause of their turning; it is their own authentic decision to turn.

We could add what Paul says to Agrippa in defense of his ministry (Acts 26:16). God had said to Paul: "I will deliver you from the Jewish people, as well as from the Gentiles, to whom I now send you, to open their eyes, in order to turn them from darkness to light, and from the power of Satan to God, that they may receive forgiveness of sins and an inheritance among those who are sanctified by faith in Me" (Acts 26:17–18). This passage clearly infers that unbelievers would have their eyes opened *before* turning away from darkness, in order to receive the forgiveness of God. Romans 9:17 also refers to Pharaoh who, having chosen to harden his heart against the Lord, became nevertheless a means of displaying God's glory. Pharaoh's heart was willfully obstinate long before the Lord confirmed him in his intractable stubbornness, in order to fulfill His purpose of delivering, with great signs and wonders, the Hebrews from slavery in Egypt: "But Pharaoh hardened his heart at this time also; neither would he let the people go" (Exod 8:32).

Incidentally, this account in Exodus is not dealing directly with the issue of the redemption of either the Egyptians or of the Hebrews led out of Egypt by Moses. For instance, this passage says nothing about the eternal destiny of the slain firstborn of Egypt, some of whom would have been infants. Is it not amazing that whatever wickedness men may plan, the Lord remains in overall charge and how, even in judgments, He turns events to good for His glory and people's redemption? The crucifixion of Jesus is the supreme example of how God brings endless good from man's rebellion and wickedness.

"If anyone wills to do His will, he shall know concerning the doctrine, whether it is from God" (John 7:17). He never hinted that people would not come to Him because of some predetermined choice made by His Father in heaven: "But you *are not willing* to come to Me that you may have life" (John 5:40; italics mine). Neither in these passages, nor anywhere else in Scripture, is there the slightest hint that it is God's responsibility to make us willing by "prevenient grace" in order for us to desire Him and enjoy His fulfilling His will in our lives. Of course He meets us with the essential help and enabling of His wonderful grace as we prepare to take our first step towards Him.

God abhors sin. So how then could He bring Himself to predestine unilaterally its eternal perpetuation in anybody? Would that not resemble more the sovereignty of a tyrant than of a benevolent ruler? Let us rest assured that all individuals are, in every sense, genuinely responsible for their own persistence in a life of sin and unbelief, and there has never been, nor will there ever be, any failure on God's part sincerely to keep His offer of life open to all.

7

Is Everybody Able to Repent?

IT IS NOW TIME to ask ourselves this question: Did our Sovereign Lord design automatons; puppets that He would at all times completely control, or did He establish in people the ongoing ability freely to respond to exhortations to seek and serve Him, having preserved in them this basic volitional ability after the Fall? Indeed, we need to ascertain whether or not it is true that people can freely respond to the exhortation to seek Him, casting themselves upon His mercy and becoming, through faith, members of "the household of God" (Eph 2:19). The Bible contains innumerable obvious instances of invitations to all men to turn to God. How can we all heed this imperative command, "God now commands all men everywhere to repent," found in Acts 17:30?

Is this command to repent sincere, as well as sobering? By saying "all men," could God just mean us to understand "all kinds" of men? Greek vocabulary is certainly not lacking in words for "all kinds." Paul speaks of different kinds of tongues in 1 Corinthians 12:10, and in 1 Corinthians 14:10 he again refers to all sorts or kinds of languages, or voices, in the world. Furthermore, if God really did mean "all kinds" of men, then would not the Holy Spirit have inspired the writer to simply say so in Acts 17:30, quoted above? We can safely conclude that this is not what He meant, and that God's command to repent is for everyone, everywhere.

Webster's dictionary defines repentance, in religious usage, as: "To feel so contrite over one's sins as to change, or decide to change, one's ways."[1] Could a person be justly condemned for failing to repent and believe if he or she was utterly incapable of doing so? Since God makes His mercy and grace accessible to all, that grace, if availed of, will impart to each individual the capacity to repent and believe in response to His com-

1. *Webster's*, 1234.

mands. "For God has committed them all to disobedience, that He might have mercy on all" (Rom 1:32). Is this some sort of divine double-talk? God forbid! It is indeed an entirely sincere and reliable statement. With kind indulgence, God the Father, because of Jesus, has been constantly willing to overlook so much sin committed in plain ignorance. "Truly, these times of ignorance God overlooked, but now commands all men everywhere to repent" (Acts 17:30).

If we are not all free to repent, because some of us have been supposedly "passed over" by God, then this command to "all men everywhere" to do so would make no sense. It would be like a prison guard inviting a group of chained detainees to come and fetch their food, but then only capriciously unchaining a select few of them to actually do so, "passing over" the others.

It is worthy of note that in the original Passover, it was God's "passing over" that *spared* from judgment and condemnation those who chose to obey Him by putting lamb's blood on the lintel and doorposts of their dwellings. (See Exodus 12:22.)

There is nobody on earth to whom the call to repent does not apply. God makes His enabling grace available to everyone, making it possible for them to turn to Him, except in the case of those who have persistently resisted God's call to the point of irreversible hardness of heart. However, in order to be saved, each individual person needs to respond freely to this grace, simply because, as we said, God sovereignly chose to allow man to conserve his genuine, autonomous freedom of choice. Jesus commands us, in Mark 16:15, to preach the gospel to every creature. What is this gospel, this very good news, if it is not that Christ died for the sins of the whole world, not just the sins of an elected few? Those of us who one day will experience the joys of heaven will be there because, with God's grace and help, we freely and positively responded to the message of salvation, and not because we had been picked out in eternity past as the selected objects of a mysterious divine choice.

Calvinism, together with Lutheranism, appeals to Isaiah 6:9–10 as proof that the unregenerate human heart cannot even want to seek after God. But what does that passage actually teach us? "And He said, 'Go and tell this people, keep on hearing, but do not understand; and keep on seeing, but do not perceive.' Make the heart of this people dull, and their ears heavy, and shut their eyes; lest they see with their eyes, and hear with their ears, and understand with their heart, and return and be healed.'" If total depravity, in the sense given to it by TULIP theology, was an accurate statement of fallen man's condition, it would be unnecessary for God to commission the prophet to make the heart of the people fat and their ears heavy. According to TULIP, they would already be in that condition! These were Israelites who had so hardened their hearts, through a constant rejection of God's message, that they had placed themselves beyond the possibility of conversion and healing. Jesus too said similar things concerning those who had deliberately turned their backs on His message of reconciliation.

We have the same situation just before the flood in Genesis 6:5 where God says of man, "Then the Lord saw that the wickedness of man was great in the earth, and that every intent of the thoughts of his heart was only evil continually." Now if TULIP were correct, what else could God hope to see? Here again it is speaking of almost all mankind having reached a point where confirmed, hardened hearts were beyond all possibility of change. This condition is in contrast to the situation prior to that, and it explains why God sent the flood at that particular time to destroy mankind. Had the earth's population become completely and irremediably corrupted before then, God would possibly have sent the flood even earlier, since His holiness and justice will not allow evil to go beyond the limits that He Himself has established. Taking all of Scripture into account, and not just selected passages, let us allow both sound judgment and passion for truth to prevail among us all, with the love of Christ in evidence as we seek to glorify Him and search the Scriptures to ascertain what they really do say.

Most importantly, how can we understand and interpret the Old Testament if we disregard the truth that God's people were free either to obey or to disobey and follow other gods, and that God was forever wooing His people back to Him? "Can a virgin forget her ornaments, or a bride her attire? Yet My people have forgotten Me days without number" (Jer 2:32). God's relationship with His people *always* carried conditions they had to fulfill, as exemplified in Jeremiah: "But this thing I commanded them, saying, 'Obey My voice, and I will be your God, and you shall be My people; and walk in all the ways that I have commanded you, that it may be well unto you.' But they hearkened not nor inclined their ear, but walked in the counsels and in the imagination of their evil heart, and went backward and not forward" (Jer 7:23–24). Is it conceivable that God would command people to walk in the way of His commandments if many of them were incapable of doing so by divine choice? (See also Isaiah 1:16–20 and Malachi 3:7.)

If our God had already fixed our personal destiny by some eternal and unchangeable decree, general calls to repentance would, for many, be a mockery. Could you imagine a loving God being capable of that? No indeed! It is up to us to heed His warning call and choose to obey Him: "Today, if you will hear His voice, do not harden your hearts, as in the rebellion" (Heb 3:15). The Lord Jesus Christ is eager to help us repent and will increase our capacity to do so if we will but ask Him. Second Timothy 2:25 says, "In humility correcting those who are in opposition, if God perhaps will grant them repentance, so that they may know the truth."

Repentance involves change within both heart and mind. A new and different disposition of heart produces a different way of thinking, leading to significant, and hopefully permanent, changes in behavior. We find a key to a fuller understanding of the word "repentance" in the following passage: "yet when they come to themselves in the land where they were carried captive, and repent, and make supplication to You in the land of those who took them captive, saying, 'We have sinned and done wrong, we have committed wickedness,' and when they return to You with all their heart and with all their soul . . ." (1 Kgs 8:47–48).

Isaiah cries out on God's behalf, "Look unto Me, and be saved, all the ends of the earth; for I am God, and there is none other" (Isa 45:22). What other possible meaning could have been in Isaiah's heart, if there were some people in any remotest corner of the world who were inherently unable to look unto God? How could God appeal to the ends of the earth to look to Him for salvation if there was no reliable provision of it available to all?

There is no hint in the Old Testament that God withheld the grace needed for any man to turn from his wicked ways and follow Him. However, as we saw, God can certainly withdraw grace from persistently rebellious souls. The tragic story of Esau serves as a warning to those who deliberately turn away from God. (See Hebrews 12:17.) One must receive the truth as it stands, and not minimize, limit, or try to explain away these wonderful invitations from God.

In spite of these clear statements of Scripture, a noted Calvinist theologian and author explains free will this way: "To be morally responsible man needs only the capacity for choice, not the freedom of contrary choice. . . . Human beings voluntarily choose to do what they do. The fact that God has foreordained human choices and that His decree renders human actions certain does not therefore negate human choice."[2] I hope you have understood this. I haven't! Another well-known Calvinist asserted that, "God so controls the thoughts and wills of men that they freely and willingly do what He has planned for them to do."[3] Do you share my difficulty in grasping the accuracy, meaning, and usefulness of the above quoted statements?

In Isaiah 55:7, we notice that the call goes out to the wicked to forsake their way and to turn to the Lord. The unmistakable implication is that the wicked are indeed able to do such a thing. Let us admit that the Isaiah passage demonstrates that the forsaking and turning *precede* God's mercy, and not the other way round, as most Calvinists would have us believe: "Let the wicked forsake his way, and the unrighteous man his thoughts; let him return unto the Lord, and He will have mercy upon him, and to our God, for He will abundantly pardon."

The view of most church fathers of the first three centuries was certainly different to that of Calvin regarding what Adam lost through the Fall. It was clear for Chrysostom (347–407) that God, having placed good and evil in our power, has given us full freedom of choice as to our response. Even earlier, Origen (185–254) maintained that free will is part of our natural reasoning powers, to enable us to discern between good and evil.

The Bible teaches conclusively and emphatically that man still possesses the freedom to choose or reject God. This is epitomized in Deuteronomy 11:26–28: "Behold, I set before you today a blessing and a curse: the blessing, if you obey the commandments of the Lord your God which I command you today; and the curse, if you do not obey the commandments of the Lord your God, but turn aside from the way which I command you today, to go after other gods which you have not known." (See also Luke 4:56 and Matthew 11:28.)

In Acts 5:31 Peter says of Jesus, "Him God has exalted to His right hand to be Prince and Savior, to give repentance to Israel and forgiveness of sins." Repentance and forgiveness were offered to all of them, not just to a selected few, but not all accepted this wonderful gift. It would hardly be consistent with God's revealed character for us to imagine that He could

2. Henry, *God, Revelation*, 84–85.
3. Boettner, *Reformed Doctrine*, 222.

state that He is not willing that any should perish (see 2 Peter 3:9), and, at the same time, select just some people to exercise repentance and faith. How could any sinner suffer from an inherent inability to receive God's gift of eternal life, and then be punished with eternal condemnation for failing to do so? Incidentally, the above quote from the book of Acts, regarding God giving repentance to Israel, makes one realize that Peter and John Calvin disagreed on another matter! Remember that, according to Calvin, God first has to give regeneration before anybody can repent or experience full forgiveness. Surely, if Calvin was correct here, Peter, instead of mentioning repentance and forgiveness of sins, would have said, in Acts 5:31, that God would first grant them regeneration, in order that they might then experience repentance and forgiveness! Unfortunately for Calvinists, that is not what this Scripture says.

Repetition can get tedious, but this matter of the universality of the gospel message deserves extra emphasis. In the following verse "whoever" is surely the key word: "To Him all the prophets witness that, through His name, whoever believes in Him will receive remission of sins" (Acts 10:43). The ability of every person to believe the gospel is absolutely implied in Mark 16:15: "And He said unto them, 'Go into all the world, and preach the gospel to every creature.'" Nowhere in this context does it say *all kinds* of people! Scripture also says, "He who believes and is baptized shall be saved; but he who does not believe will be condemned" (Mark 16:16).

Jesus promised He would send the Holy Spirit to "convict the world of sin" (John 16:8). Why would Jesus send the Holy Spirit to convict the world of sin if, in fact, people were utterly incapable of doing anything other than continuing in sin, and God the Father had the intention of only providing to some picked-out ones the potential means of escaping sin's clutches? Notice that the text puts the responsibility squarely on man to choose to believe. The context here is "the world." In the same breath Jesus refers to the "ruler of this world" and the Spirit's ministry of convicting the "world." Are we to put two different meanings on the word "world" in the same statement? Jesus does not say men *cannot* come to Him but that they *will not*: "And you will not come to Me, that you might have life" (John 5:40). If they do not come, it is because they will not come. They certainly could come if they wanted to, unless they had so persistently resisted the Lord's voice as to harden their heart beyond remedy, as we said earlier. It is also mentioned in Hebrews 3:15: "Today, if you will hear His voice, Do not harden your hearts as in the rebellion." It is certainly not God who has made them unwilling. Why would He? Can you think of any reason at all why our God, who is "Love," would choose to leave them in an unwilling state by divine decree? Our heavenly Father is infinitely more merciful and generous than any earthly authority, more so than you or I could possibly imagine. "For He is kind to the unthankful and evil. Therefore be merciful, just as your Father also is merciful" (Luke 6:35–36).

William MacDonald has a very helpful comment on Matthew 13:11–12: "Because it has been given to you to know the mysteries of the kingdom of heaven, but to them it has not been given. For whoever has, to him more will be given, and he will have abundance; but whoever does not have, even what he has will be taken away from him." MacDonald writes:

> The disciples had faith in the Lord Jesus; therefore, He would give them the capacity for more. The Jewish nation . . . had rejected the light . . . therefore . . . they would lose what little light they had. Light rejected is light denied. It was simply the outworking of a principle built into all of life—willful blindness is followed by judicial blindness. They were unwilling to understand the wonderful fact of the Incarnation.[4]

I would like to remind you at this point of just how generous and merciful is our God.

Our heavenly Father is infinitely more merciful and generous than any earthly authority. He offers His forgiveness to whoever is willing to receive it.

When the priest of Jupiter (Zeus) wanted to make sacrifice to Paul and Barnabas, this is how the apostles pleaded with the priest and the multitude: "Men, why are you doing these things? We also are men with the same nature as you, and preach to you that you should turn from these useless things to the living God, who made the heaven, the earth, the sea, and all things that are in them" (Acts 14:15). Are these the words of apostles who believed that people could take no steps at all to forsake

4. MacDonald, *Believers' Bible Commentary, New Testament*, 70.

idolatry, unless God intervened in their wills? Were it so, would not Paul have said something like this: "Look men, we know that you are helplessly lost and unable even to want to turn to the living God, so we are now going to plead in prayer, in anticipation of our Heavenly Father granting some of you the ability to turn to Him"? Nothing of the sort! What would even be the sense of this imagined prayer if they were predestined to hell? No amount of pleading with God could change anything. If Paul did not think they could take steps to forsake idolatry, he would not even imagine that his prayers could change their predestination "unto doom or salvation." Similarly, we can look at Paul's reply to the Philippian jailer in response to his question in Acts 16:30–31: "Sirs, what must I do to be saved?" Paul answers: "Believe on the Lord Jesus Christ, and you will be saved, you and your household." Here we see belief first, and salvation afterwards as a result of that belief, not as the cause of it.

Let us remember that even after we have been instructed in righteous living, we can then turn from it, disproving any notion that there is a clear, eternal distinction between those who are "chosen" and those who are not. We see this in 2 Peter 2:21, which reads: "For it would have been better for them not to have known the way of righteousness, than, having known it, to turn from the holy commandment delivered unto them." In the following quote, the order of things is very evident, with no hint of the granting or withholding of "prevenient grace" from God: "If My people, who are called by My name, will humble themselves and pray, and seek My face, and turn from their wicked ways, then I will hear from heaven, and will forgive their sin and heal their land" (2 Chr 7:14). The call went out to disobedient Israelites to choose to humble themselves, pray, seek God's face, and turn from evil, before God would hear, forgive, and intervene.

We can add these clear statements concerning our part and then God's part in deliverance: "As I live, says the Lord God, I have no pleasure in the death of the wicked, but that the wicked turn from his way and live. Turn, turn from your evil ways; for why should you die, O house of Israel" (Ezek 33:11)? How would we fit the following verse about wisdom into the Calvinistic scenario?

> Because I have called and you refused, I have stretched out my hand and no one regarded, because you disdained all my counsel, and would have none of my rebuke, I also will laugh at your calamity; I will mock when your terror comes, when your terror comes

like a storm, and your destruction comes like a whirlwind, when distress and anguish come upon you. Then they will call on me, but I will not answer; they will seek me diligently, but they will not find me, because they hated knowledge and did not choose the fear of the Lord." (Prov 1:24)

How could souls who disdained wise counsel and refused to heed warnings suddenly decide diligently to seek God? If they were totally depraved in the Calvinistic sense, such seeking would be impossible. Alternatively, if God were in fact moving their hearts to seek Him, He would have allowed them to find Him. Let us face it, this is yet another passage that just does not fit TULIP.

God calls us to seek Him, so how can we interpret Romans 3:11 within this spirit of freely seeking God: "There is none who understands; there is none who seeks after God"? This verse originally described a specific situation in Israel and not a universal one, for it is a quote from Psalm 14:2 that reads: "The Lord looks down from heaven upon the children of men, to see if there are any who understand, who seek God." Why would the Lord even bother to look down to see, if all of humanity were "totally depraved," unwilling, and unable to seek God? What would be the point? I would appeal here for some balance in interpreting and applying Paul's quote from Psalm 14.

There are very many references concerning man seeking God. In the above quote from Romans 3:11, Paul is merely reinforcing the fact that, since we are all infected with and affected by sin, although not all to the same intensity, nobody seeks God for Himself, at all times with his whole heart, in humility and faith. The words of Jesus in Matthew 7:13–14 ought to prove conclusively that everyone is free to choose the way of repentance unto life. There, Jesus exhorts people to "enter by the narrow gate." Why would He do that if God had fixed in advance the gate by which the individual would choose to enter?

Having emphasized the responsibility of everyone on earth to choose the way of repentance, it is nevertheless very necessary to keep things in balance by reminding ourselves again that we are, in every sense, dependent creatures, and that of ourselves, without God's enabling, we do not possess the power to follow through on our desire for full communion with Him. However, in order to fulfill His gracious purposes, He has chosen to preserve perpetually our genuine human freedom of choice. The following verse epitomizes the theme running throughout all of Scripture: "If you seek Him, He will be found by you" (1 Chr 28:9). It is tragic, but true, that the kingdom of heaven's delights remain veiled to all those who refuse to acknowledge their own need of repentance.

8

Did Jesus Choose Whom He Would Save?

M OST CALVINISTS TEACH THAT we did not freely choose to follow Jesus, but that we were constrained to respond to God by some irresistible compelling on His part. They say that it was by God's choosing that we were picked out for salvation, and even try to prove it with verses like, "You did not choose Me, but I chose you and appointed you that you should go and bear fruit, and that your fruit should remain, that whatever you ask the Father in My name He may give you" (John 15:16). However, this "being chosen" has more to do with the function and vocation of the apostles than with their salvation. Jesus chose the twelve from among the many who followed Him, and they in turn were eager to leave all for His sake. The meaning of chosen here would be similar to that in John 6:70, where Jesus says, "Did I not choose you, the twelve, and one of you is a devil?" If Jesus had chosen Judas for eternal life, how could the text say, "Satan having entered into him" (Luke 22:3)? He had chosen Judas and the other eleven as apostles, not elected them as believers, otherwise Jesus would also have saved Judas; so this choosing referred to their specific ministry and service for God, rather than to salvation itself.

We could think of it in terms of a football club manager and trainer. Players have freely chosen to request membership in the club, and from that reserve of members, the trainer chooses those who will play in the next match. The trainer knows the capabilities of his players, so there is of course an element of foreknowledge in his choices. In a similar vein, Jesus picked men out for apostleship from amongst the many who chose to follow Him, with the element of foreknowledge obviously also playing a part.

The Bible clearly refers to Jesus as the One supremely chosen by God the Father: "Behold My Servant, Whom I have chosen, My Beloved, in whom My soul is well pleased! I will put My Spirit upon Him, and He will declare justice to the Gentiles" (Matt 12:18). Obviously, this chosenness has nothing at all to do with the certitude of Jesus' eternal destiny! This passage refers to the special redemptive mission He was destined to accomplish, leaving heaven's glory to live here on earth and then make atonement for the sins of the whole world.

In Acts 22:14, when Paul was arrested in Jerusalem, he gave a significant account of what Ananias had said to him after his conversion experience. Ananias spoke of God having chosen Paul to know God's will, to see the Just One, and to hear the voice of His mouth. This is certainly to do with God having chosen him for apostleship, not to the salvation experience itself. God had chosen Paul for a particular ministry, and he would become a witness to all men revealing what he had seen and heard, transmitting instruction to the churches as led by the Holy Spirit, and thus creating outstanding pages of divinely inspired Scripture.

One might well ask how to interpret the following verse: "But we are bound to give thanks to God always for you, brethren, beloved by the Lord, because God from the beginning chose you for salvation through sanctification by the Spirit and belief in the truth" (2 Thess 2:13). Now if this verse stopped at the word "salvation," we could all be in trouble! However, Paul does not stop there, but goes on to emphasize that God's chosen way for entering into life is not through trusting in our good works, but through the sanctifying work of the Holy Spirit, and by our believing the truth concerning the Person and atoning work of the Lord Jesus, who is the Truth. (See John 14:6.) It is the Spirit who sanctifies, and we then have to work out in our daily lives, in the words of Philippians 2:12–13, what God has worked in, applying ourselves with concentration and dedication to the transforming process. Once we have set our heart upon God, He pours out His abundant grace to enable us to make the choices that contribute to our becoming more like the Lord Jesus.

Incidentally, an earlier verse in 2 Thessalonians explains plainly why people perish. It is referring to God having chosen us to benefit from a specific quality of life, rather than speaking of whether any specific individual does or does not possess that life.

> The coming of the lawless one is according to the working of Satan, with all power, signs, and lying wonders, and with all unrighteous deception among those who perish, because they did not receive the love of the truth, that they might be saved. And for this reason God will send them strong delusion, that they should believe

the lie, that they all might be condemned who did not believe the
truth, but had pleasure in unrighteousness. (2 Thess 2:9–12)

Notice that this verse says absolutely nothing about some previous divine
decree to exclude or damn anybody. The condemnation comes solely because of unwillingness to receive the love of the truth.

Again, the children of Israel are God's chosen people, but who would
take this to mean that they are all saved? Jesus Himself stated that this is
not the case: "And I say unto you, that many will come from the east and
west, and shall sit down with Abraham, Isaac and Jacob in the Kingdom of
Heaven. But the sons of the Kingdom will be cast out into outer darkness.
There will be weeping and gnashing of teeth" (Matt 8:11–12). In Romans
2:9 Paul rejects the idea that national election was a pledge of national
salvation. We read in Deuteronomy 7:7 about God calling Israel to an
earthly role that brought great opportunities for blessing, and Jacob's offspring had done nothing to merit such a role in human history. The tragic
refusal of many Israelites to repent of their disobedience and idol worship
brought great dishonor on God's name.

Let us remember that New Testament Greek originally had no punctuation, so translators have to be very careful about choosing and placing
punctuation marks in order to give the correct emphases. Consequently,
the sense of some Scripture passages has not always been correctly conveyed, most notably in the Vulgate, a translation into Latin by Jerome in
the fifth century, and the old Geneva Bible of 1560. These early translations
contained textual and copying errors that were transmitted through the
years and adversely affected some subsequent versions. The old Geneva
Bible, a revision of Tyndale's, published during Calvin's rule in Geneva,
was not only heavily influenced by the Vulgate but also slanted towards
Calvin's own theology, and it contained copious notes written by Calvin
himself. It was this Geneva Bible that first introduced the division of the
text into chapters and verses, and many successive editions appeared, even
after the publication of the King James Version in 1611. This latter version
leaned heavily, in addition to other earlier translation attempts, upon the
work that produced the Geneva Bible, and this is enough to explain its
noticeable Calvinistic bias. Contemporary scholarship has now enabled
us to further our comprehension of many Greek words and to correct
errors. However, certain difficulties of interpretation still remaining make
one wary of dogmatism concerning some more difficult texts.

It is important to emphasize that one cannot cast doubt on the plain meaning of the vast majority of texts just because of the remarkably few which may continue to challenge our comprehension. To give just one example, Acts 13:48 could read: "And as many as had been *appointed* to eternal life believed," rather than *ordained* as in the KJV. The verb "been appointed" is in the past passive tense and it can have several meanings, including to be "submitted," "put in order," "appointed," or "fixed." Giving a preferred translation is not altogether straightforward. Of course, the believers are indeed destined for eternal life.

Incidentally, the entire episode in Acts 13:38–48 gives no support at all to determinist Calvinist ideas. Paul addresses all who fear God (v.26), assures them that everyone who believes is forgiven (v.38), urges them to continue in the grace of God (v.43); and the opposing Jews are condemned for thrusting aside the Word of God and judging themselves unworthy of eternal life (v.46). Acts 2:47 also mentions "those who were being saved," and not "such as should be saved" as in the KJV, and this amendment has solid scholarly support. There is nothing here to contradict the numerous clear texts already cited.

Therefore, in the light of the facts of the original New Testament Greek's lack of punctuation, and of the text not having been originally divided up into chapters and verses, one can readily understand the scope there is for divergent translations. Very easily one's theological bent influences one's interpretation, since to some extent we all bring our prejudices to the Bible text. How true it is that "He that complies against his will is of his own opinion still."[1]

We believe unreservedly that the Holy Spirit verbally inspired the original writings, and most of us know that none of the earliest manuscripts have been preserved, leaving us dependent upon copies of copies that differ from one another in many minor instances. Nowadays there are increasingly effective means of comparing different sources and manuscripts, notably through the facilities afforded by computers. Thanks to the progress that has been made, all of us can benefit from research in such areas as punctuation and shades of meaning, and can confidently enjoy our favorite Bible translation. Indeed, it can be very enriching to refer to other translations, and to see how alternative ways of expressing a passage of Scripture bring something into better focus. Let us remember to thank

---

1. Butler, *Hudibras*, lines 547–48.

God for His faithfulness in watching over His Word down through the centuries, giving us such reliable and trustworthy Bible versions.

9

Is Grace Ever Irresistible?

THE COUNCIL OF DORDT (1618–19), from which TULIP doctrine was formulated, sought to maintain that God's grace only comes to those whom He chose in advance for eternal life. This Council decided that saving (or enabling) grace could not be resisted because it is God Himself who changes rebellious hearts so that those—and only those—thus changed can not only want to believe on Him, but cannot do otherwise. However, is this what the Word of God actually teaches?

Theologians differentiate between common grace and saving grace. Defining each can be very helpful. Common grace principally refers to all of God's kind infusion of benevolent creative power in the universe, from the inconceivably vast regions of outer space right down to the life cycle of the tiniest microbes on earth. God, through and by Jesus Christ, His eternal Son, as stated in Hebrews 1:3, is the Creator, Sustainer, and Upholder of all of life. Saving grace describes His redemptive activity in the world, seeking to bring people into intimate relationship with Himself. Through God's mercy, common grace and saving grace overlap and intertwine. He constantly deploys both His common and His saving grace in our world to provide the means whereby He can draw all people to Himself, although not all people choose to respond to His drawing.

In John 6:44 Jesus said, "No one can come unto Me unless the Father who sent Me draws him." Let us note that there is a difference between "wanting to come" to Jesus and actually possessing the power to come to Him. This verse is not saying that no one can want to come to Jesus unless His Father who sent Him draws Him. We will always need empowering from God in order to approach Him, but what we are saying is that God reaches out in grace and mercy to all who freely want to come. Jesus said, "And I, if I am lifted up, will draw all peoples to Myself" (John 12:32). The Greek text omits the word "people" so that it reads: ". . . will draw *all* to Myself " (italics mine). Most translators have inserted either "men," "people," or "peoples." Who then are these "all"? Jesus did not limit the term just to the Jews and Greeks in John 12:20, or only to the chosen ones, some men, or even many men, but by saying "all," Jesus' words are indeed all-embracing. He did not die only for kings, presidents, and theologians, but for ordinary people, some of whom are illiterate or barely literate, so surely He would choose words that would enable them to understand that this drawing to the Father includes them. The context confirms the plain meaning of these words, reminding us again that God desires to include everybody in His offer of the saving grace that would enable them to enter into living relationship with Him, through repentance and faith.

Some maintain that the Greek word used for "draw" in John 12:32 means an irresistible dragging that can apply only to the elect. However, the Greek verb used does not restrict the drawing to the elect. The same word is used for drawing a sword. It is a verb that does not even hint at irresistibility and no well-informed, honest scholar would say it does. However, in Matthew 13:47–51 we read:

> "Again, the Kingdom of Heaven is like a dragnet that was cast into the sea, and gathered some of every kind, which, when it was full, they drew to shore, and they sat down and gathered the good into vessels, but threw the bad away. So will it be at the end of the age. The angels will come forth, separate the wicked from among the just, and cast them into the furnace of fire. There will be wailing and gnashing of teeth. Jesus said to them, 'Have you understood all these things?' They said unto Him, 'Yes, Lord.'"

Have *we* understood? This passage uses a different Greek verb with a similar meaning for "draw." Both good and bad fish (the just and the wicked) are drawn into the net. Does this honestly fit the Calvinist concept of Jesus only meaning His drawing all *kinds* of men to salvation in John 12:32? We know that Jesus was perfectly able to express the idea here of "all kinds," but He did not, so we can conclude that "all" simply means "all" in Scripture, unless the immediate context begs for a modified meaning.

In Acts 14:19, we read of the Jews in Antioch "dragging" Paul out of the city, and the Greek word used here has the notion of irresistible force, sometimes with violence. Hauling in the net of fish in John 21:6 uses the same Greek word as in John 12:32, so "drawing all men" employs a much less violent word than the one used in Acts 14:19 when Paul was dragged out of the city, and in Acts 17:6 where Jason and some brethren are dragged before the rulers. If Jesus wished to convey such a violent, irresistible idea in John 12:32, He could have used this more forceful Greek word.

Perhaps we should add a further word concerning what Jesus meant by "All that the Father gives Me will come to Me, and the one who comes to Me I will by no means cast out" (John 6:37). He did not say "all that the Father draws to Me," but "gives Me." It is always important to notice what a verse does not say. Since this passage says nothing about the motivating factors or reasons behind the Father's gifts to His Son, we cannot use this statement to support the TULIP view of election. Here, Jesus reminds us again that He is in full submission to His Father, warmly receiving all who willingly come to Him; all whom the Father gives Him. "This is the will of Him who sent Me, that everyone who sees the Son and believes in Him may have everlasting life" (John 6:40). Jesus draws all men to Himself but not all want to come. What can be said of the following: "No one can come to Me unless the Father who sent Me draws him; and I will raise him up at the last day" (John 6:44)? This is an instance where Jesus mentions the Father's drawing, but implies no idea of irresistible attraction. Of course, none of us can come unless God bestows upon us His amazing grace.

We read in Romans 5:18: "Therefore as through one man's offense, judgment came to all men, resulting in condemnation, even so through one Man's righteous act the free gift came to all men, resulting in justification of life." Judgment came to all men and the gift of life also came to all men, in the sense that no men are outside the range of its availability. What kind of exegesis would allow one meaning for "all" in the first part of the verse, but a different meaning for "all" in the second part? The following verse says nothing to contradict this affirmation, "For as by one man's disobedience many were made sinners, so also by one Man's obedience many will be made righteous" (Rom 5:19). Here we see the word "many" applying equally to both sinners and the righteous. Applied to sinners, we know that the "many" refers to all members of the human race, not just some, "For all have sinned and come short of the glory of God" (Rom 3:23). Similarly, its use in "many will be made righteous" must also mean that the potential is there for all members of the human race to be made righteous in Christ with His imputed righteousness. Paul adds that where sin increased, grace abounded even more (Rom 5:20). What could he mean, other than that God offers His abounding grace, the pathway to right standing with God, even to the vilest offenders? How tragic that so many choose to resist and refuse Him!

Quoting John 17:9, some maintain that here is proof that Jesus did not die for the whole world: "I pray for them. I do not pray for the world but for those whom You have given Me, for they are Yours." However, the immediate concern of our Lord in this prayer is certainly not a denial of His love for the world, but a deep concern for His own disciples as He prepares to leave them. One could just as easily misinterpret Jesus' meaning when, in John 16:26, He says, "In that day you will ask in My name, and I do not say to you that I shall pray the Father for you, for the Father Himself loves you, because you have loved Me, and have believed that I came forth from God." Here Jesus is introducing the disciples to a new and thrilling dimension in their life of prayer, as He gets them ready for His physical absence. They will then go straight to the Father with their worship and requests, using Jesus' Name. He is not negating the fact that He constantly asked things for His disciples, and Hebrews 7:25 reminds us that Jesus continues to intercede for them. One cannot start formulating doctrine from sayings that have their context in a particular setting, time, and place, rather than in a general one.

None of us has done anything to merit God's grace (His enabling), and all of us are utterly and thoroughly dependent upon His mercy. Our only reticence in defining "grace" as "unmerited favor" would be because we read: "The Child [Jesus] grew and became strong in spirit, filled with wisdom; and the grace of God was upon Him" (Luke 2:40). Jesus could hardly experience His Father's *unmerited* favor! We also read in Hebrews 2:9: "we see Jesus, who was made a little lower than the angels, for the suffering of death crowned with glory and honor, that He, by the grace of God, might taste death for everyone." Grace is, of course, wholly undeserved for us sinners, yet God chose to lavish His enabling and empowering grace upon us, something we could not possibly earn, and without which we would remain separated from Him. Someone has composed a helpful acronym for GRACE: "God's Riches At Christ's Expense."

Speaking to Jews who were willfully resisting the work of God's spirit, Stephen, the first Christian martyr, said, "You stiff-necked and uncircumcised in heart and ears! You always resist the Holy Spirit; as your fathers did, so do you" (Acts 7:51). Resisting the work of God's Holy Spirit is just another manifestation of "resisting his grace." Here is a very plain statement that God's grace is not irresistible. Not only is this very clear evidence that God's grace is not irresistible for unsaved people, but there is nothing in the Bible about God's grace being irresistible for "the elect."

What does the Bible actually say? "We then, as workers together with Him also plead with you not to receive the grace of God in vain" (2 Cor 6:1). If you can receive God's grace in vain, then it cannot be as irresistible as some teach it to be! If God's grace were irresistible for anyone, the following exhortations would be meaningless: "How shall we escape if we neglect so great a salvation, which at the first began to be spoken by the Lord and was confirmed to us by those who heard Him" (Heb 2:3)? Here is a stern warning for us to be watchful: "Beware, brethren, lest there be in any of you an evil heart of unbelief, in departing from the living God, but exhort one another daily, while it is still called 'today,' lest any of you be hardened through the deceitfulness of sin. For we have become partakers of Christ if we hold the beginning of our confidence steadfast to the end" (Heb 3:12–14).

If God's grace were irresistible for unbelievers, would it not be equally so for those who have received Christ? Yet, as Christians, how often we fail to obey God and do all His will! So how could His grace be irresistible for those not yet His children, and then cease to be irresistible once we have become His children? In practice, we need to ask constantly for fresh outpourings of His grace as we seek to cope with the challenges of life. "Let us therefore come boldly unto the throne of grace, that we may obtain mercy, and find grace to help in time of need" (Heb 4:16).

Similarly, when God calls us to a specific ministry for Him, we are just as capable of refusing as of accepting the grace that God makes available with the call. When God called Moses to one of the most significant and dramatic ministries in Hebrew history, he was at first very reticent about obeying. Moses was God's chosen link in the chain of deliverance from bondage, yet he made excuses about his own ability to negotiate with Pharaoh on God's terms. Moses's brother, Aaron, unlike Moses, had no such royal background. He had been raised with his own people and would most probably have only learned enough everyday Egyptian, with an unpolished accent, to dialogue with the slave drivers. In contrast, Moses spoke very refined Egyptian learned from infancy at the palace, and he would have understood the subtleties of court conversation; although after forty years of relative solitude minding sheep, he now felt shy and most inadequate. (See Exodus 4:10–16.)

Aaron was not an obvious choice at all, yet Moses pleads with God to be relieved of the job! He was very clearly resisting God's available grace, and doubting its adequacy to equip him for the task. We can see that Moses had not yet acquired a disposition of great eagerness for obeying God during this long training period lasting forty years in the wilderness. Is there any real support here, or anywhere else in Scripture, for the idea that grace would be irresistible in any aspect of God's dealings with man?

"God is love" (1 John 4:8), and He is also sovereign in the true, biblical sense of the word. He is also perfectly just, which rules out any notion that the Word portrays an eccentric, absolutist monarch capriciously picking and choosing whom He will single out for salvation. Yet this, in plain words, could sum up Calvin's view of enabling grace.

To add a word concerning God's wrath, Isaiah 28:21 (KJV) describes it as "His strange work." This is simply because His character is principally one of loving-kindness and mercy, and nobody anywhere has been mysteriously excluded from this tender mercy. "The Lord is good to all, and His tender mercies are over all His works" (Ps 145:9).

It is lovely to see how Paul and Barnabas speak to the crowd in Lystra, in Acts 14:17, portraying God as kind and merciful, delighting in showing mercy to bygone generations, doing good to all, not just to some: "Nevertheless He did not leave Himself without witness, in that He did good, gave us rain from heaven and fruitful seasons, filling our hearts with food and gladness." Earlier the prophet Micah exulted in the character of God: "Who is a God like unto You, pardoning iniquity, and passing over the transgression of the remnant of His heritage? He does not retain His anger forever, because He delights in mercy" (Mic 7:18), and, of course, the Psalms overflow with praise for the wonderful blessings of the God we serve.

Now if grace were "irresistible," why would the apostle Paul labor in prayer for his lost compatriots? What could his prayers change? If God had damned unbelieving Jews by divine decree, what would have been the use of Paul interceding for them? Yet no one would doubt that Paul was in touch with the Holy Spirit as he expressed his longing to see his countrymen saved! "Brethren, my heart's desire and prayer to God for Israel is that they may be saved" (Rom 10:1). We are sincerely moved by how deeply he cared: "I tell the truth in Christ, I am not lying; my conscience bearing me witness in the Holy Spirit, that I have great sorrow and continual grief in my heart. For I could wish that I myself were accursed from Christ for my brethren, my countrymen according to the flesh" (Rom 9:1–3). How could Paul intercede for the lost with such fervor if he was not completely convinced that God, for His part, yearned to save all of them, if only they would respond to Him? The same applies to us in our intercessory life.

Let us catch the wider, vaster vision of our generous God's extensive redemptive activity in the entire world, inspired by His desire to bless mankind, regardless of how little we deserve His kindness. We can even fit suffering of various kinds into this universal framework of abundant grace, enabling us to embrace trials of whatever sort with unshakable confidence in Him.

We can confidently conclude that there is no such thing as "irresistible grace," either before or after salvation, and we can all lean on the abundance and sufficiency of God's available grace in every circumstance of life.

10

What Kind of Sovereignty Does God Have?

B EFORE SEEKING TO ANSWER this question, let me state categorically that I hold a very high view of God's sovereignty. I believe wholeheartedly that God is forever and eternally in overall control of His universe. Nothing escapes Him and nothing can happen without His permission, nor is He limited in His abilities and power. One of my dearest hopes is that this book will help enhance our appreciation of God's sovereign ways.

In what sense is God's sovereignty similar to earthly sovereignty? Is His sovereignty different in essence, or in extent, or both? If God's sovereignty is different in essence, for example, to Queen Elizabeth II, then surely a different word should be used, or coined, to avoid misunderstanding. Queen Elizabeth is the sovereign ruler of the British Commonwealth of Nations, whereas God is the sovereign ruler of the universe. What are the similarities and differences? Let us stick to Webster's definition of sovereign: "Above or superior to all others; chief, greatest, supreme. Supreme in power, rank or authority; of or holding the position of ruler, independent of all others."[1]

Borrowing words in everyday use and giving them a different application can be suspect. I mentioned already that some Calvinist theologians take the liberty of redefining words. This is a very serious problem in that it can come dangerously close to sophistry, which is defined in Webster's as "unsound or misleading, but clever, plausible and subtle argument or reasoning"[2]

Some Calvinists can unwittingly portray God as an absolutist, despotic sovereign. According to them, He can torture His subjects on earth

1. *Webster's*, 1395.
2. Ibid., 1391.

and then in hell forever, to suit His own good will and pleasure, and nothing a person can do will change his torturous destiny, unless the Sovereign Lord decides unilaterally to intervene.

Whilst bearing in mind that God is both sovereign and omniscient (knowing all things), in order to explain clearly what the Bible means by "Sovereign Lord," it is fitting to take human examples from everyday life. Has any earthly sovereign ever been held directly responsible for all the acts and antics of his or her subjects? Does Queen Elizabeth organize and control every detail of the lives of any or all of her citizens? Are her Prime Ministers able successfully to do so? Even tyrannical rulers have never been able to do this, yet we speak of their sovereignty. Furthermore, what kind of earthly sovereign would one most expect people to love and revere? Need we even ask if it would be the absolutist, tyrannical sort of monarch who rules despotically, or the kind, benevolent, and caring type who longs for happiness in his subjects, and constantly watches over their well-being without oppressively curtailing their liberties? We can similarly ask ourselves to what kind of sovereign ruler of the universe we would most readily submit and offer our loving devotion?

What then was John Calvin's own stated view of God's sovereignty? In his *Institutes of the Christian Religion*, we find the following:

> Nothing is more absurd than to think anything at all is done but by the ordination of God . . . every action and motive of every creature is so governed by the hidden counsel of God, that nothing can come to pass, but what was ordained by Him . . . the wills of men are so governed by the will of God that they are carried on straight to their mark which He has foreordained.[3]

Such was our brother Calvin's conviction regarding the way God reigns over mankind! Where does this absolutist idea of sovereignty come from? Notice the insertion of his idea of "hidden counsel" concerning God's manner of ruling. Who then propagated the notion that God in heaven wills, orders, directs, and controls absolutely everything that humans decide and do? Certainly, God's Word, taken as a whole, does not teach this, and this strange idea does not correspond with the world in which we actually live. Of course God sees and knows all, including the wicked and perverse things that humans choose to do, but He cannot, and must not, be held in any way responsible for all the pride, rebellion,

---

3. Calvin, *Institutes,* vol.1, 234–35.

injustice, and perversity in the world. The earthly events that God directs are not necessarily the foreordained actions of specific pre-determined individuals, but things that He strategically organizes to fulfill His overall purposes in furthering the objectives of His kingdom.

When we speak of God's sovereignty, we must be careful to define it in terms of what the Bible in its entirety reveals about His character and ways. Once the Father has restored us to intimate fellowship with Himself through our believing Christ's reconciling work on our behalf, we can enjoy a very vivid sense of right and wrong, of justice and injustice. Wise earthly rulers govern by delegating responsibilities, with their subordinates enjoying a certain pre-determined area of freedom of decision and action. These earthly power structures are but a shadow of how God has organized the universe. There are heavenly principalities and powers, some loving and serving God wholeheartedly, and some antagonistic to Him, but these powers are nevertheless subordinate to God's grand overall plan of redemption. Ephesians 6:12 says, "For we wrestle not against flesh and blood, but against principalities, against powers, against the rulers of the darkness of this age, against spiritual hosts of wickedness in the heavenly places." Notice in this text that we wrestle—not that we merely endure and submit to being on this battlefield, or that we inactively count on God being in control—but we fight. God wants us all to be vigorously involved in the cosmic battle, and positively deployed in strategic ministry. Sadly, many saints are not functioning as warrior saints at all. In their everyday lives, the good fight has deteriorated into a quest for the good life. The cost in lost spiritual effectiveness is incalculable.

God is all-powerful, yet lovingly self-restraining. He could control everything, but He chooses not to. If God created all things for Himself, then it is His obvious desire that through grace all created things be reconciled to Him, the only obstacle being our free choice to refuse to seek the way of full obedience and abundant life in Him.

We find a good example of the principle of divine delegation of responsibility in Genesis 18:25: "Shall not the judge of all the earth do right?" Many believers will quote this verse to appease honest inquiry into the destiny of the unevangelized, but this passage conveys another significant insight into God's ways: "And the Lord said, 'Because the outcry against Sodom and Gomorrah is great, and because their sin is very grave, I will go down now and see whether they have done altogether according to the outcry against it that has come to Me; and if not, I will know'"

(Gen 18:20–21). Then the two angels proceeded to Sodom to uncover, on the Lord's behalf, the extent of the population's sin. What is the point of this investigative episode if the spirit of sovereign delegation is set aside when it relates to our divine Sovereign's ways? Are we to discard such illustrations of divine delegation as simply examples of primitive Hebrew religion?

The Psalms are full of cries for God to establish His justice in the earth. What would be the point, if God had already fixed everything from eternity? "Oh, let the wickedness of the wicked come to an end, but establish the just; for the righteous God tests the hearts and minds" (Ps 7:9) Why would the psalmist expend energy crying to God like this, if He had already fixed everything in advance? Obviously, the psalmist felt that he could touch God's heart through his supplications, and obtain protection from his enemies. Abraham's intercession is also a potent reminder that we can touch the Father's heart and help change the flow even of major events. James 5:17 draws attention to the change in the weather in response to Elijah's prayer, the inference being that, by the grace of God, we also are able to do such a thing.

Nowhere in Scripture does it say that Jesus gave up the sovereignty He shared with His Father, while He took on human form on earth. Philippians 2:7 says Jesus "emptied himself" or "made himself nothing," but the context does not really explain it. In Charles Wesley's hymn beginning "And can it be that I should gain an interest in the Savior's blood?" he says in the third stanza that Jesus "emptied Himself of all but love," but does this accurately convey what Paul meant? It is certain that the Bible nowhere states that Jesus gave up His sovereignty whilst on earth. Undoubtedly, by His own choice, and in submission to His Father, He refrained from exercising it in quite the same way as before His incarnation. Jesus was God incarnate on earth, sovereignly ruling over the elements, stilling winds and storm, supernaturally healing many sick, and miraculously feeding the five thousand. At no time did He stop being God, even when on the cross He bore our iniquities; and the heart of God's masterful redemptive plan is surely the fact that He Himself would pay for all of our sins. However, even though "in Him dwells all the fullness of the Godhead bodily" (Col 2:9), we read of limits to His works of mercy. It is stated in Mark 6:5 that "He could do no mighty work there . . . and He marveled because of their unbelief." Was their unbelief in Nazareth indeed able to hinder Jesus' work, accomplished in complete dependence upon His

Father? This is strange language in which to portray "sovereignty" in the Calvinist sense of the word! One of Jesus' titles on earth is "Lord" and He always acted in conjunction with His Father, as He explained, "I can do nothing of Myself" (John 8:28). Lordship explicitly implies sovereignty. Remember, Jesus continued to show forth all of God's character whilst on earth, for "He that has seen Me has seen the Father" (John 14:9). Yet humans could hinder or help His acts of mercy!

Here is another quote from Calvin's *Institutes*:

> God not only foresaw that Adam would fall but also ordained that he would. I confess it is a horrible decree; yet no one can deny but God foreknew Adam's fall, and therefore foreknew it because He had ordained it so by His own desire.[4]

Is not the suggestion astounding, that our beloved Father in heaven could have actually wanted Adam and Eve to fall and that He wished them to do the very thing He had commanded them not to do regarding the fruit from the forbidden tree—that eating it was His plan and desire? Is this teaching not frankly illogical, inconsistent, and unworthy of God's character? Calvin certainly missed some essential facets concerning God's dealings with fallen beings like Adam, Eve, Cain, Abel, Seth, and Enosh, so let us look more closely at how He lovingly dealt with these people.

First of all, we need to notice that God did not distance Himself in an indignant mood of aloofness or resentment when our first parents disobeyed Him. He remained close by these two fearful and self-conscious people, clad in their fig leaves. God, in his profound grief, did not retreat into offended silence. He reached out to Adam and Eve, asking some very pointed questions. Of course, our omniscient God already knew the answers. He looked into their human hearts and knew what desires and longings were hidden within them, including the sinful ones. However, He asked Adam the following kind questions: "Adam, where are you?" (Gen 3:9), and "Who told you that you were naked? Have you been eating from the tree which I forbade you to touch" (Gen 3:11)?

Why would God ask such questions when, after all, He knew the whole situation perfectly? What can we learn from this dialogue? Most importantly, we notice that Adam missed the opportunity to confess his disobedience and repent of it. Instead of saying, "O Lord, what have I done? I've been so wrong and disobedient! I implore You to forgive me,"

4. Calvin, *Institutes*, vol. 3, 568–69.

Adam said, "The woman whom You gave to be with me, she gave me of the tree, and I ate" (Gen 3:12). Adam blamed his wife. How easy to do, but what barriers to blessing such behavior creates! Perhaps there is a hint of reproach here towards God, as the One who created this wife who had listened to Satan. Was God now giving Adam a chance to think about what he had done? (Incidentally, nowhere does this passage speak either of an apple or of any sexual misdemeanor, as many people seem to think.) When He turned from Adam to talk with Eve, He asked her, "What is this you have done?" (Gen 3:13), and with a reply typical of fallen human nature, Eve chose to pin the blame on somebody, or something, else—in this case the serpent, who had not a leg to stand on!

Therefore, in asking these kind questions, time and space were being given to both Adam and Eve in which to repent and express godly sorrow for the way they had grieved His heart with their foolishness. God designed these questions to help them, and followed with His practical intervention on their behalf by lovingly making them leather garments (Gen 3:21). His kind attentions brought some very significant responses. We read: "Now Adam knew Eve his wife, and she conceived and bore Cain, and said, 'I have acquired a man from the Lord'" (Gen 4:1). Eve could so easily have said, "Look how clever I am, I've produced a baby boy!" Instead, she gave God the credit, acknowledging that He was the giver of life. We see this again in Genesis 4:25, where "Adam knew his wife again, and she bore a son and named him Seth, 'For God has appointed another seed for me instead of Abel, whom Cain killed.'" Eve was at last responding fully to the gentleness and kindness of her Creator. Later, after Seth had a son he named Enosh, "men began to call on the Name of the Lord" (Gen 4:26). Eve was undoubtedly God-conscious and giving Him the glory, and men were now calling upon the Name of the Lord. Where is this supposed removal at the Fall of even the desire to seek God, as taught by John Calvin?

Notice that God did not curse Adam and Eve for having sinned. God only cursed the ground and the serpent. However, we see in Genesis 4:11 that Cain was cursed after killing his brother Abel, having deliberately committed a dreadful act of murder—the destruction of a beautiful masterpiece of God's creation. Cain knew that his conduct deserved death, but God in mercy deferred the full punishment. It could be that God was granting Cain an opportunity to repent as he experienced His kindness and protection. If that was so, he did not choose the way of repentance, but rather a life of wickedness.

Given man's ongoing ability to choose either right or wrong, sin was inevitable. No, God did not plan the Fall, contrary to what Calvin would have us believe. Fortunately, in His love and wisdom, the Lord had fully provided for the advent of sin. Although it is altogether true that God is wrathful towards all the unrighteousness of those who persistently ignore Him, He remains tender, loving, gentle, and kind to all who sincerely repent and seek His face. These very kind dealings between God and our earliest forebears, and their responses to His mercy and goodness, do not in any way confirm the statements of Calvin or the declarations of the Council of Dordt (1618–19), Article 3, Section 3, where they maintained that all men are conceived in sin and born as children of wrath, incapable of anything good, bent towards evil, dead in sin, and slaves of sin. They said that without *first* receiving regenerating grace, men cannot even desire to change, cannot turn to God, and can do nothing towards correcting their depraved nature.

Furthermore, according to Calvin, nothing we do—or fail to do—can in any way thwart God's sovereign purposes in "election unto salvation." To be strictly logical, why then would we even bother to be involved in the task of evangelism if all those sovereignly "chosen" by God will inevitably be redeemed through the irresistibility of His grace, whether we seek to win them or not? It would indeed be hard to obey enthusiastically the command to go and make disciples of all nations, as recorded Matthew 28:19–20, if we believed that it could all happen anyway without our involvement.

God is all-powerful, yet lovingly self-restraining. Because He is sovereign, He certainly could control everything men do, but He chooses not to. For instance, Peter points out, when dealing with Ananias's lies in Acts 5, that having sold some property, it is Ananias himself who remains in control. "While it remained, was it not your own? And after it was sold, was it not in your own control? Why have you conceived this thing in your heart? You have not lied to men but to God" (Acts 5:4).

Having created all things for Himself, God desired that by His grace all people be reconciled to Him, the only obstacle being the exercise of their freedom to refuse to seek the way of obedience and abundant life.

Psalm 78:41 says, "Yes, again and again they tempted God, and limited the Holy One of Israel." How could they limit God in the exercise of His sovereign actions, unless He chose to allow them a very real degree of control over their attitudes and affairs, as with Ananias cited above? This verse states explicitly that they could and did, which reinforces the conclusion that some of Calvin's teaching on the nature of God's sovereignty is seriously in error.

To a Calvinist, for whom God's sovereignty would be demeaned by the admission that man can and must freely choose to respond to God's offer of salvation, we must ask the following question: Would not His sovereignty also be diminished by the need for Christians to freely choose to continue to walk in God's way? Yet, as believers, we work out our relationship with Him in godly fear and trembling, cooperating with Him in the ongoing process of sanctification. This element of our active participation is a recurrent theme in Scripture: "As you therefore have received Christ Jesus the Lord, so walk in Him: rooted and built up in Him, and established in the faith, as you have been taught, abounding in it with thanksgiving" (Col 2:6–7). For instance, we learn to flee from certain temptations, since God is not going to do the fleeing for us: "Flee also youthful lusts; but pursue righteousness, faith, love, peace with those who call on the Lord out of a pure heart" (2 Tim 2:22). God does not do what He calls us to do in the working out of our practical transformation. He has an unlimited and all-sufficient supply of help there for us to draw on at all times in our pursuit of holy living, but we ourselves have to learn the discipline both of availing of His help, and of applying ourselves to obeying His commands. Paul speaks of ". . . the exceeding greatness of His power toward us who believe, according to the working of His mighty power . . ." (Eph 1:19). With such a provision of God's help available, we need not face with any apprehension a verse such as this: "Therefore, my beloved, as you have always obeyed, not as in my presence only, but now much more in my absence, work out your own salvation with fear and trembling; for it is God who works in you, both to will and to do for His good pleasure" (Phil 2:12–13). This verse reminds us of just how much our walk with God is a partnership, and that nothing is automatic in practical experience.

Paul reminds us that we have the will to do good but that apart from the Holy Spirit we do not have the power: "For I know that in me (that is, in my flesh) nothing good dwells; for to will is present with me; but how to perform what is good, I do not find" (Rom 7:18). He does not say, "in my flesh dwells no good thing, not even the desire to seek God." Nowhere do we read in Scripture that we, with our sinful nature, lack the ability to want to seek God. Of course, as we said, we will always need God's abundant grace in order both to seek and find Him, and then to walk in obedience to Him. Indeed we will!

We must also guard against neglecting or dismissing the teaching of the Old Testament, where God constantly appeals to the Israelites to return to Him. Denying their complete freedom to do so renders the following text meaningless: "O that they had such a heart in them that they would fear Me, and always keep all My commandments, that it might be well with them, and with their children for ever!" (Deut 5:29). How else are we to understand quotes like this where God expresses His longing for the Israelites, His chosen people, to experience a change of heart, they alone bearing full responsibility for their personal conduct, uncircumscribed by any supposed selective divine choice? We can conclude that such statements of Scripture confirm neither Calvin's understanding of God's sovereignty nor his dismissal of man's genuine ability to choose to turn to God.

If, as sinners, we are unable to want to seek God, why would Hosea and Joel exhort us as follows: "Sow for yourselves in righteousness, reap in mercy, break up your fallow ground; for it is time to seek the Lord, till He comes and rains righteousness on you" (Hos 10:12)? According to the spirit of what Calvin wrote—though at times he did contradict himself—the Israelites would actually have been unable to sow, reap, break up fallow ground, and seek God. However, this verse indicates that they were well able to do this, which is why the Lord of Hosts appealed to them in this manner.

What does Jesus mean when He says to His disciples in John 14:30, "The ruler of this world is coming, and he has nothing in Me"? To whom was He referring? In 2 Corinthians 4:4, Paul describes Satan as "the god of this world" and portrays him as having definite usurped powers. The apostle John writes of the great usurper in these words: "We know that we are of God, and the whole world lies under the sway of the wicked one" (1 John 5:19). What a relief to be reminded that Jesus came to "destroy the works of the devil"! Clearly, this infinitely evil spirit is a sufficient threat to our well-being for Jesus to address the fact, and to focus on our learning by His strength in us to overcome the very real power that Satan possesses. John reminds us, "He who sins is of the devil, for the devil has sinned from the beginning. For this purpose the Son of God was manifested, that He might destroy the works of the devil" (1 John 3:8). Paul gives the similar warning, quoted earlier, "For we do not wrestle against flesh and blood, but against principalities, against powers, against the rulers of the darkness of this age, against spiritual hosts of wickedness in the heavenly places. Therefore take up the whole armor of God, that you may be able to withstand in the evil day, and having done all, to stand" (Eph 6:12–13).

Satan does indeed rule in many hearts, and can perform great wonders, as exemplified in the contest between Moses and Pharaoh in Exodus chapters 5–10. The book of Revelation teaches us that as this present age draws to a close, Satan will deploy his wicked demons in ever more powerful supernatural attempts to thwart God's pure and perfect plans. However, he is unable to operate outside limits set by God Himself.

The suffering of Job is a case in point. God did not choose the methods by which Satan would torment Job, Satan did (Job 1:12). Again, some believers appeal to statements made by Job's comforters to bolster up the absolutist sovereignty issue. Job's comforters had many fine things to say about God and His ways, yet God called upon them to repent of their attitudes and of what they had said to His servant Job. ". . . you have not spoken of Me what is right, as My servant Job has" (Job 42:8).

The universe is still waiting for the day when God's purposes are consummated, as is made clear by the following passages: "For we know that the whole creation groans and travails in pain together until now" (Rom 8:22), and ". . . whose minds the god of this age has blinded, who do not believe, lest the light of the gospel of the glory Christ, who is the image of God, should shine on them" (2 Cor 4:4). In Revelation 11:15 we read, "The kingdoms of this world have become the kingdoms of our Lord and of His Christ, and He shall reign forever and ever." Obviously, until this culminating event, "the kingdoms of this world" could not be described as "the kingdom of our Lord." Therefore, it is important that we identify what we mean when we use the term "divine sovereignty," and our understanding of it must absolutely fit in with all that the Bible has to say about it.

The sovereign desire of the Lord of heaven is to establish a kingdom filled with His love.

Let no notion, however appealing, rob us of the fact that God does not only love immeasurably, He *is* love (1 John 4:8, 16). We cannot force others to love us. True spiritual love flourishes and prospers in a climate of genuine freedom and liberty, not in one of coercion.

We must also ask ourselves whether the outcome of events is always according to God's sovereign will, since passages like Isaiah 46:9–12 have been used to try to prove that all of God's will is always inevitably done on earth:

> Remember the former things of old; for I am God, and there is no other; I am God, and there is none like Me, declaring the end from the beginning, and from ancient times the things that are not yet done, saying, "My counsel shall stand, and I will do all My pleasure," calling a bird of prey from the east, the man that executes my counsel, from a far country. Indeed, I have spoken it, I will also bring it to pass; I have purposed it, I will also do it. "Listen to me, you stubborn-hearted, who are far from righteousness."

Yes, God's counsel would stand, and what He sovereignly decided would indeed happen. However, this did not mean that God dictated the responses and actions of each individual involved. God can certainly choose to employ men in their rebellious state to fulfill His purposes, especially in chastisement. Even so, how could God ask the stubborn-hearted to listen to Him if in fact they were unable to do so? In Jeremiah 3:22 God pleads, "Return, you backsliding children, and I will heal your backslidings. Indeed, we do come to You, for You are the Lord our God." He asks them to choose to return, and the result would be the healing of their backsliding. God does not say, as some would have it, that He would sovereignly heal them, and as a result of that healing they would return to Him.

In Jeremiah 4:1–4 God pleads again with His rebellious chosen people:

> If you will return, O Israel, says the Lord, Return to Me; and if you will put away your abominations out of My sight, then you shall not be moved. And you shall swear, "The Lord lives," in truth, in judgment, and in righteousness; the nations shall bless themselves in Him, and in Him they shall glory. For thus says the Lord to the men of Judah and Jerusalem: Break up your fallow ground, and do not sow among thorns. Circumcise yourselves to the Lord, and take away the foreskins of your hearts, you men of Judah and inhabitants of Jerusalem, lest My fury come forth like fire, and burn that no one can quench it, because of the evil of your doings.

If these people were in fact helplessly "dead in their sins," how then could they break up the ground and remove the foreskin of their heart. How could they even hear God speak? The answer is, as I explain in chapter 12, that you cannot take "dead in sins" as a literal analogy with physical death.

Clearly, the grace of God has forever been available to all men and He is no respecter of persons. No favorites! No arbitrary exclusions! No mystery here! Remember too that we had a specific, not a general, situation in Genesis 6:5, where God says of man that "every intent of the thoughts of his heart was only evil continually." This condition was in contrast to how things prevailed in previous times, and explains why God sent the flood at that time to destroy mankind. Since God is perfectly just, if men had completely corrupted the earth before this time, He would probably have already sent the flood. Do you not think this obvious? Is it not deeply troubling how some Calvinists seem to snatch so many verses out of their context? Let us solemnly challenge them to a careful and honest approach to these matters.

> *Be reassured of this basic fact:*
> *there is only one true gospel, which is*
> *the message of God's redemptive love for all mankind.*

In the Lord's Prayer, Jesus told the disciples to pray that God's will be done on earth, a pointless petition if God's will is indeed always done. In Psalm 9:19 we find this cry: "Arise, O Lord, do not let man prevail; let the heathen be judged in Your sight." This shows that the psalmist certainly did not share the view that God's will always prevails. To say that God directs all details of what happens on earth is to make Him an accomplice in rape, violence, theft, lies, murders, and the passing of laws that allow the murder of millions of unborn children. This brings us back to the fact that our Sovereign Lord has purposed that man be free to choose between righteousness and evil behavior, since His grace is available to all.

Unquestionably, the grace of God has been forever accessible to all men. Again, many Calvinists use the following verses to promote the view that God rules as an absolutist sovereign on earth: "And all the inhabitants of the earth are reputed as nothing; and He does according to His will in the army of heaven, and among the inhabitants of the earth. No one can restrain His hand or say to Him, 'What have You done'" (Dan 4:35)? This statement in the book of Daniel by a contrite pagan monarch can hardly be used to buttress any doctrine concerning God's sovereignty. It does remind us, however, that our Sovereign Lord could be recognized, even by a non-Jew with a past steeped in idolatry, as leading the affairs of nations. Monarchs, whatever might be their perverse ambition, cannot become actual absolute rulers. Just as God has set limits on Satan's activities, likewise He has set all-wise limits upon all humans. Man's folly cannot outwit, or prevail against, the Most High.

Our prayers and pleadings can indeed influence God's dealings with men, but He always reserves for Himself the final word. In practice, the Lord seems frequently to grant nations the leadership they most crave in their wilful blindness. Where humble intercession prevails on behalf of a nation, God can respond by giving better leadership than the nation deserves. Such was the case with America's founding fathers. The colonists were a very mixed bag, yet President George Washington set the tone with his uprightness and integrity. Another outstanding incidence of divine mercy in national leadership was the efficacious conjunction of King George VI and Winston Spencer Churchill guiding the British Commonwealth of Nations throughout World War II.

Contrary to much Calvinistic thinking, God does not control everything a monarch decides to do. In this respect, the family unit ought to serve as a good illustration of the principle at stake. I am head of our home, yet I have no desire, calling, or need to control my wife. Freedom and complete loving trust are the effective operating principles, because the basic bond is one of Christian love, not coercion. Christian family life is meant to reflect, however dimly and inadequately, God's order and operating principles in the universe. Love, daily prayer together, and living in integrity and loyalty keep the family unit close, and so it is with our Heavenly Father and His children. He urges our intercession for governors, since the world would enjoy a vastly improved moral environment if only we Christians took much more to heart the ministry of intercession for the authorities of this fallen world. (See 1 Timothy 2:1.)

With the psalmist, we should all acknowledge that the earth rightfully belongs to God, "For the kingdom is the Lord's, and He rules over the nations" (Ps 22:28). In the same vein, Jesus taught His disciples to pray, "Thy kingdom come" (Matt 6:10), reminding us that God's absolute rule is still in the future.

Our Father in heaven is altogether mindful of the smallest details of human existence. This is quite different from saying that He directly controls them all, although He could if He so wished. When Christians say, "Oh well, God is in control," they can, in fact, be expressing a deep misinterpretation of the meaning of the term. If we will trust in the Lord with all of our heart, according to Proverbs 3:5–6, consciously commit our ways to Him, and humbly request His intervention, then we might justifiably say that God is now in control of our life and our situation. However, to imagine that God is automatically going to control and correct every circumstance in our life, however careless we might be in our relationship to Him, is an unfortunate misunderstanding to which, amongst others, Calvinists are prone.

When Jesus speaks of His Father's will in Matthew 10:29, He is referring to His permissive will. Why number the hairs on our head? For some, this may have become no longer possible, but for all of us, it is exquisitely comforting to know that God's order reaches right down into our molecular makeup, and that all our physical attributes or defects can be graciously accepted from His hand. All of creation is in bondage to physical dying and death because of the Fall. This is what Romans 8:20–22 says:

> For the creation was subjected to futility, not willingly, but because of Him who subjected it in hope; because the creation itself also will be delivered from the bondage of corruption into the glorious liberty of the children of God. For we know that the whole creation groans and labours with birth pangs together until now.

This present worldwide condition of things is, above all, a reflection of God's permissive will. It is neither His absolute nor His consummate will. One day there is going to be a brand new heaven and a perfect new earth, wherein those clothed in the Lord's righteousness will enjoy the glorious liberty of undistractedly serving their glorious Redeemer. Tragically, all rebels will spend eternity in outer darkness, and the Word of God is straightforward and emphatic on these points.

Let us again pause to thank God for the way that the Holy Spirit wonderfully enabled the writers of Scripture always to express themselves in a way that conveyed, to ordinary people, exactly what they were sovereignly inspired to impart.

Most importantly, how can we understand and interpret the Old Testament if we deny the fact that it reveals a God forever wooing His people back to Him, and that they are free to obey or to disobey and follow other gods? "Can a virgin forget her ornaments, or a bride her attire? Yet My people have forgotten Me days without number" (Jer 2:32). The Lord appeals to the Israelites to choose to obey, in order to enjoy His blessing. Tragically, the Israelites so often chose not to heed their Lord.

> But this thing is what I commanded them, saying, "Obey My voice, and I will be your God, and you shall be My people; and walk in all the ways that I have commanded you, that it may be well with you." Yet they did not obey or incline their ear, but followed the counsels and the dictates of their evil hearts, and went backward and not forward. (Jer 7:23–24)

Is it conceivable that God would command the Israelites to do all these things if in fact, as in the following quote, they were incapable of doing them? "Look unto Me, and be saved, all the ends of the earth, for I am God, and there is none other" (Isa 45:22). What other possible meaning could have been in Isaiah's heart, if all over the world people were inherently unable to look to God? How could God appeal to all the people on earth to be saved if there was no available offer of provision for all of them to be saved? There is no hint in the Old Testament that God had withheld the grace needed for men to turn from their wicked ways and follow Him. Let us receive the truth as it stands and not minimize these wonderful invitations from God.

In Leviticus 19:5 we learn about bringing free will offerings to the tabernacle. The essence of this word is explicit. An Israelite was free to choose to honor God willingly or to go after other gods. Quite clearly, God's grace was at all times available to enable the Israelites to obey the Lord.

If we take away genuine human freedom of choice, we empty of sense all the flow of Old Testament history.

What could be more obvious than that the chosen people had very real autonomous choices set before them. "I call heaven and earth as witnesses this day against you, that I have set before you life and death, blessing and cursing: therefore choose life, that both you and your descendants may live" (Deut 30:19). Here is epitomized the very spirit of the Old Testament relationship between Israel and the Lord: "Sanctify yourselves therefore and be holy, for I am the Lord your God. You shall keep my statutes and do them: I am the Lord who sanctifies you" (Lev 20:7). I would suggest that you now read 1 Samuel 12:13–15 and ask yourself if these verses fit the Calvinist scenario.

The New Testament follows on from the Old, so at what point in the record of God's dealings with man would people cease to possess the freedom to choose? Do we not rob God of sovereignty if we deny Him the liberty to grant to all human beings the gift of genuine freedom of choice, in the sense in which ordinary people understand these terms.

Above all, we see the true nature of God's sovereignty at work in the matter of prophecy. God masterfully governs His universe despite human disobedience, keeping watch over the flow of history, so that He can always fulfill His prophetic Word and accomplish His strategy for bringing salvation to the ends of the earth. Let me assure you of this basic fact: the gospel is the sublime message of God's redemptive love for all mankind.

11

What Is Foreknowledge?

WEBSTER'S DICTIONARY DEFINES FOREKNOWLEDGE as "knowledge of something before it happens or exists; prescience."[1]

Since some confusion exists over its implications, it will help us to consider how we humans experience foreknowledge. We "foreknow" that when autumn comes many trees will drop their leaves. We also "foreknow" that when our children reach the age of seven or eight their smile will display a gap or two followed by some nice new teeth. Does this foreknowledge in itself make us responsible for the event? Of course not! We know in advance that if we drop a hen's egg on the ceramic tiled floor, it will break, so we try to avoid doing so. We do, in fact, foreknow numerous things and make plans accordingly, sometimes making contingency plans. God is also able to lay contingency plans!

Some Christians think that God cannot have foreknowledge of future events unless He is also the cause of them, but this is false reasoning. In Acts 2:23 we read about God's "determined purpose and foreknowledge." Clearly, foreknowledge is a separate concept to determined purpose. The latter is another way of saying, "decisions taken in accordance with all the facts." God possesses foreknowledge of many things, like sinful acts, which He in no way desires or plans. It is very reassuring to know that, in the words of Ephesians 1:6, and despite our sins, those of us who love and serve God are "accepted in the Beloved." This is in spite of all the imperfections of which the Lord had unmistakable foreknowledge when, before the Fall, He established our high calling by adopting us as sons into His family through the work of Jesus Christ.

Created in His image, we experience partial and restricted foreknowledge of events in the future, but God experiences such foreknowl-

---

1. *Webster's*, 566.

edge in a complete and unlimited sense. Our very limited abilities in the area of planning for the future make it hard for us to grasp how God can coordinate things for our ultimate good in the midst of human rebellion and sin. God has locked us all into time and space, and we attempt to look from here into a realm that is beyond the scope of our finite minds, whereas God has no such limitations. Since we can only speculate what it must be like for God to be outside of the restrictions of time, it is best to leave the matter with Him, resting in the assurance that in spite of His perfect foreknowledge, He certainly did not desire or plan everything that happens on our sin-sick earth.

The following verse in Isaiah has troubled some folk, but it is saying that when man persists in resisting God's plan, He allows calamity to strike: "I form the light, and create darkness: I make peace and create calamity: I the Lord do all these things" (Isa 45:7 NIV). We need to make the clearest distinction between what God desires and what He permits. Our Sovereign Lord permits Satan, the god of this world, to be a source of unfathomable evil. In addition, the wickedness of man's unregenerate heart leads him to live outside God's desire and purpose for him. However, God asks, "'Do I have any pleasure at all that the wicked should die,' says the Lord God, 'and not that he should return from his ways and live'" (Ezek 18:23)? God will help men to repent, but in no manner will He force repentance and a change of direction upon them.

God's "determinate counsel," decisions based upon all the facts, is also something that we can only grasp in a very limited manner. As Proverbs 19:21 puts it: "There are many plans in a man's heart, nevertheless the Lord's counsel—that will stand."

In the following verse, God's foreknowing and foreordaining (or predestining), are two separate and distinct elements, although they work together for our good. "For whom He foreknew, He also predestined to be conformed to the image of His Son, that He might be the firstborn among many brethren" (Rom 8:29). Although this verse says that God foreknew, it does not say what he foreknew. Nor does it necessarily speak of specific individuals, but rather of that numberless crowd who would choose to receive Him, since they are the ones destined to become like Jesus. We notice a distinction made between "determined purpose" and "foreknowledge" concerning Jesus' death on the cross. The Bible speaks of Him as "being delivered by the determined purpose and foreknowledge of God . . ." (Acts 2:23). Purposing something is different to merely foreknowing it, since the former involves both planning and fulfilling something settled in advance.

As we said, with our finite understanding, we find it impossible even to begin to conceive of the total and complete nature of God's infinite knowledge. With well over six billion people living on planet earth, how can we possibly grasp the immensity of the fact that He sees into the heart of each individual and knows its secrets? We desperately need to get away from the determinist thinking that has blighted some sections of the church for so long, and instead, acknowledge that the Lord is a feeling Being, who responds both in love and in wrath to human attitudes, decisions, and situations.

Incidentally, God chooses to forget sins confessed and forsaken: "For I will be merciful to their unrighteousness, and their sins and their lawless deeds I will remember no more" (Heb 8:12). He no longer remembers! Similarly, God could, if He so wished, choose not to know certain future events, in order to sustain the element of surprise. However, nothing can be hidden from His gaze, and 1 Chronicles 28:9 shows the futility of thinking otherwise: "As for you, my son Solomon, know the God of your father, and serve Him with a loyal heart and with a willing mind; for the Lord searches all hearts and understands all the intent of the thoughts. If you seek Him, He will be found by you; but if you forsake Him, He will cast you off forever."

12

What Is Our Main Contention?

THE WORD OF GOD clearly teaches us that in His sovereignty God created a non-coercive universe in which He has preserved, despite the Fall, man's genuine and autonomous freedom of choice. Everybody on earth has the freedom to respond, either positively or negatively, to God's outpouring of grace.

Imagine a man in love wanting so desperately to have his feelings reciprocated that he seeks out some potion that will make his beloved return his love. This would be alchemy, smacking even of sorcery, yet many contend that God mysteriously puts, as it were, a "potion" of love for Himself in those He has beforehand chosen to redeem. Common sense should teach us that if we are to love God and be compassionate to others, then full, genuine freedom of choice, not manipulation, must prevail.

Romans 11:32 says, "For God has committed them all to disobedience, that He might have mercy on all." So are we to interpret the last "all" of the sentence differently to the first "all"? What inconsistent exposition that would be! Neither does He say "that He might have mercy on some." Surely, we believe in the verbal inspiration of the Scriptures! The Holy Spirit could easily have inspired Paul to write "some" instead of "all," but He did not. In Titus 2:11 we read: "The grace of God that brings salvation has appeared to all men." Why does it not say, "has appeared to the elect" or just "to men"? Would it say what it does not really mean? God offers mercy to all, but, tragically, not all respond positively.

When does "all" mean "all without distinction" or "all without exception"? In this matter, how easily one can set aside exegesis for "eisegesis," which is interpreting a text by reading into it one's own ideas! There are Greek words in Acts 15:9 and 1 Corinthians 14:7 that mean "distinction." The question remains: Why did not the Holy Spirit settle the matter in favor of Calvinism, in Romans 11:32, by using such qualifying Greek words?

The Word says in 2 Peter 3:9: "The Lord is not slack concerning His promise, as some count slackness; but is longsuffering toward us, not willing that any should perish, but that all should come to repentance." Some Calvinists say that Peter is addressing himself only to Christians, so does this really mean that God is simply saying that He is not willing that any of the elect perish? How could any of the elect perish or fail to come to repentance if, according to Calvin, God alone has pre-programmed them to eternal life and His elective grace never fails? This verse does not make sense if Calvinism is right. However, the text does not say "that all the chosen should come to repentance." If the Holy Spirit meant to say just "some," the "chosen," or the "elect," or just a "remnant," would He not have said that? Nor does it say "that many should come to repentance." It says "all." God's heart of love desires that all people choose the way of repentance. As we saw in an earlier chapter, Calvin spoke of God's "secret counsel" whereby He had no intention of attempting to save millions of people. This secret council would be in opposition to His declared will. I want to assure you that in terms of His desire to save everyone, no secret counsel exists.

> *It is a golden rule of Bible interpretation that we*
> *try to refrain from reading into the text*
> *what is not in fact there.*

DOES THE FALL RESULT IN OUR BEING DEAD IN SIN?

Since all men are now by nature "dead" in sin, most Calvinists believe that nobody is capable of choosing to believe on the Lord Jesus Christ, unless God specifically and individually picked him or her out before the foundation of the world. To them He would grant the grace to believe in His Son, Jesus by regenerating them (spiritual rebirth) in order to enable them to believe in His Son Jesus.

Surely being "dead in sins" (Ephesians 2:5) does not mean that we are incapable of seeking God, any more that being "crucified" (dead!) with Christ means that we are no longer capable of sinning! (Galatians

2:20). Many passages teach that we, as Christians, have died to sin. How could this term "death" be taken literally, as in physical death, as if we as Christians were no longer capable of disobeying God? In Romans 6:2–3 we read: "How shall we who died to sin live any longer in it? Or do you not know that as many of us as were baptized into Jesus Christ were baptized into His death?" (See also Romans 6:2–8.)

We cannot take the "dead in trespasses and sins" of an unbeliever in Ephesians 2:1 more literally than the "dead with Christ" of a believer. God calls those who are "dead in trespasses and sins" to seek Him, and we, who are believers "dead with Christ," are exhorted thus: "Likewise you also reckon yourselves to be dead indeed to sin, but alive to God in Jesus Christ our Lord" (Rom 6:11). Furthermore, it says in Romans 8:10: "And if Christ be in you, the body is dead because of sin, but the Spirit is life because of righteousness." What could this mean? How can our body, as a Christian, be described as "dead"? Colossians 3:3 tells us, "For you are dead, and your life is hid with Christ in God." I repeat, this cannot mean literal death, in the way we use the term, as though we Christians were now incapable of sinning! Those who as believers are "dead" to sin can "choose to" disobey God, and by the same token those who are "dead" in sins can "want to" seek God. Earlier, in Colossians 2:20–21, Paul says, "Therefore if you died with Christ from the basic principles of the world, why, as though living in the world, do you subject yourselves to regulations—'Do not touch, do not taste, do not handle?'" Obviously, the word "died" here cannot be taken in a literal sense. Nor does it mean that our bodies cannot function to please God. A Christian has died to sin, but he must nevertheless learn to put it to death in his daily experience. We have to learn how to do this, just as we have to learn to "clothe ourselves with compassion" (Col 3:5). It is helpful to remind ourselves again of what actually happened soon after the Fall. As an outcome of the first couple's disobedience, one of the results would be eventual physical death, but nothing is said about Adam's loss of ability to seek God. God kindly dialogues with Adam and Eve, clothes them, and thereby manifests His benevolent presence. When Cain and Seth were born, Eve gave God the credit. Obviously, awareness of God had not been obliterated: "And Adam knew his wife again, and she bore a son and named him Seth, 'For God has appointed another seed for me instead of Abel, whom Cain killed.' And as for Seth, to him also a son was born; and he named him Enosh. Then men began to call on the name of the Lord" (Gen 4:25–26).

Attempts have been made to prove Calvin's views on election by expounding Acts 14:16, where it speaks of Lydia, "who worshiped God, heard us; and the Lord opened her heart to give heed unto the things which were spoken by Paul." It is like grasping at straws, and saddens my heart, to see trained theologians try to make out that this verse proves anything at all about human freedom of choice. The Lord Jesus opened up her heart to heed Paul's words, just as He works in all of our hearts to heed Him. This says nothing of what had previously transpired in Lydia's heart, though the text tells us that she "worshiped God."

In the spirit of Philippians 2:12–13, we have to learn to work out in our everyday life what God has worked in us: "Therefore, my beloved, as you have always obeyed, not as in my presence only, but now much more in my absence, work out your own salvation with fear and trembling: for it is God who works in you, both to will and to do for His good pleasure." As we daily yield our hearts and lives to God, He undertakes to help change our desires and motives, and strengthen our wills so that our purpose will be to live solely to please Him. Does our cooperation with His grace in any way diminish His sovereignty? Of course it doesn't.

Numerous New Testament passages teach that we need to cooperate actively with our loving Father in order to reach the goal of Christlikeness, and it starts with choosing to believe in Him in order for Him to count us among the redeemed. There is no hint at all in the Old Testament, let alone the New, that people cannot choose to seek God: "Choose you this day whom you will serve . . ." (Josh 24:15).

Paul makes a startling claim in Galatians 2:20 when he says, "I am crucified with Christ: nevertheless I live; yet not I, but Christ lives in me." Many of us are so used to reading such language that we do not stop and tell ourselves that the meaning cannot be literal. Paul had never been physically nailed to a cross when he said this, nor had he ceased to live. Here we have another good example of figurative language that carries a profound and vital spiritual truth. Paul knew that the way to victory was through reckoning himself dead with Jesus and resurrected with and in Him. Parallel metaphors abound, as in "circumcision of the heart" and "burial in baptism."

You might want to turn to Deuteronomy chapter 13 for further reading. As you read it through, ask yourself if the spirit of this whole passage is in harmony with the Calvinistic idea that the only reason people follow after God, as opposed to false gods, is because of prevenient grace granted by God to some but not to others.

13

How Merciful Is God?

SOME CALVINISTS HAVE SUGGESTED that if Jesus died for everybody, then much of His effort was wasted because so many spurn Him, and they add that God is not in the wasting business. This is just what some disciples said when, in Matthew 26:7, expensive perfume was poured over Jesus' head. Some said, "What a waste!" On the contrary, this was an outpouring of lavish love that could never answer to the logic of reason.

Even the natural world that God created has this phenomenon of apparent waste built into it. Take, for example, the acorns that fall from an oak tree. They are all amazing seeds, bearing the potential of wonderful new life, but only a very few ever produce a new oak tree. When we preach, not everybody, alas, pays attention to our words and benefits from them. Does this mean that the message is thereby wasted? Not at all! The preacher sincerely and authentically offers it to all who are present, but he cannot force all his hearers to heed, assimilate, and apply the teaching.

In the lovely episode recorded in Mark 10:16, little children were brought to Jesus and He gathered them up in His arms, put His hands upon them, and blessed them. Is this a picture of exclusiveness or inclusiveness? In Matthew 15:32, we read of Jesus' compassion for the crowds: "Then Jesus called His disciples unto Him and said, 'I have compassion on the multitude, because they have now continued with Me three days and have nothing to eat. And I do not want to send them away hungry, lest they faint on the way.'"

Note that Jesus extends understanding and compassion here concerning the mixed motives of the multitude; He is not judging or condemning any of them. In every group of people there are mixed motives, but whether it is groups of children or adults crowding around Him, Jesus is always full of compassion and loving-kindness towards them. Nevertheless Jesus had harsh words for specific enemies like some Pharisees. How could this fit the notion that God picks and chooses, offering no help at all to some? Our precious Lord is immeasurably rich in mercy, much more so than we could ever imagine. What purpose could be served by our trying to limit this wonderful mercy to benefiting just a predetermined group? The more folk there are who turn to Him, the more joy there is in heaven!

Withholding the offer of mercy to all, when all are equally helpless in guilt, would seem a grave falling short of the justice God requires even of humans, whose righteousness can never be more than an exceedingly poor reflection of His. "He has shown you, O man, what is good; and what does the Lord require of you but to do justly, to love mercy, and to walk humbly with your God" (Mic 6:8)? Let us also note how very rich God is in both mercy and love: "But God, who is rich in mercy, because of His great love with which He loved us, even when we were dead in trespasses, made us alive together with Christ, (by grace you have been saved)" (Eph 2:4–5). It is obedience, not disobedience, that glorifies our God, who delights in being loving and kind: "But let him who glories, glory in this: that He understands and knows Me, that I am the Lord exercising loving-kindness, judgment, and righteousness in the earth; for in these I delight" (Jer 9:24).

References to God's mercy occur well over three hundred times throughout the Bible and are spread over forty-one different books. Noticeably, mercy is a major theme of Scripture. God entering into judgment is mentioned much less than half this number of times. Statistics can be misleading, but the frequency of different themes can have some significance. A key passage in Nehemiah reminds us of just how merciful God is towards sinners. Early on, the Israelites had behaved in a very proud and provoking manner, blasphemously rebelling against God and His appointed servant Moses. They readily disregarded the miracles of deliverance God had wrought on their behalf and turned to idolatry. Nehemiah reminded a subsequent generation of just how merciful, loving, and kind God had been in response to such unfaithfulness. "But they and our fathers dealt proudly, and hardened their necks and did not heed Your commandments. They refused to obey . . . but You are a God ready to pardon, gracious and merciful, slow to anger, abundant in kindness, and did not forsake them" (Neh 9:16–17).

What a wonderful God is here portrayed, responding to man's rebellion with such kindness! This is the God we adore, the One who longs to become the friend of sinners and who draws close to the humble in heart.

On the theme of mercy, see also Psalms 86:5, 103:17, 108:4, 109:26, and 145:8. God's mercy is also the constantly recurring theme of Psalm 136.

Let us guard ourselves against imagining that God's work in the world is limited to the known activities of the professing church. We can be completely reassured that Jesus lived and died for all men, and that His offer of pardon reaches to the ends of the earth, including and embracing every human being. It is a totally genuine and sincere offer of mercy to all mankind: "For God has committed them all to disobedience, that He might have mercy upon all" (Rom 11:32). We again ask ourselves if the first "all" in this clear statement is to be interpreted differently to the second "all"? Would this be the plain meaning?

In Romans 8:32 we read of Jesus having been given up for us all. What an appropriate opportunity Paul had here to say that Jesus died only for the "elect," or only for those chosen by God! Again we see how the principle of non-coercive love prevails, with God forcing nobody into His kingdom and His preservation of each individual's freedom of choice throughout the process. For those who still have a problem with God's mercy extending over all His works, and to the whole world, I suggest that you take time now to meditate upon the following five basic texts, even learning them by heart. Jesus has paid the ransom for all the sons of men: "Who gave Himself a ransom for all, to be testified in due time" (1 Tim 2:6). God carries the eternal welfare of the whole world in His heart: "And He Himself is the propitiation for our sins, and not for ours only, but also for the whole world" (1 John 2:2). The mercy of the Lord is everlasting: "O give thanks unto the Lord, for He is good; for His mercy endures for ever" (1 Chr 16:34). Jesus did not come to earth just to be the Redeemer of a pre-selected bunch of people: "For to this end we both labor and suffer reproach, because we trust in the living God, who is the Savior of all men, especially of those who believe" (1 Tim 4:10). We call out to God, and He pours upon us His mercy: "For you, Lord, are good and ready to forgive, and abundant in mercy to all those who call upon you" (Ps 86:5). Let us note that this does not speak of God calling us to salvation, but of us calling to Him. It does not say in Psalm 86 that His extended mercy precedes man's cry for help. Our "deadness" does not limit or prevent our crying out to Him to save us from our sins.

Let us stop and take on board the comforting, universal fact that God's mercy is abundant. However, the conditions for receiving God's mercy are clearly delineated all through the Scriptures. If we choose the pathway of strict honesty and openness with God, confessing and endeavoring to forsake all known sin, we are assured that He will show us abundant mercy. "He who covers his sins will not prosper, but whoever confesses and forsakes them will have mercy" (Prov 28:13). Part of Jonah's predicament in preaching judgment upon Nineveh arose from his knowledge of how very kind and gracious God is, and that He might not do what Jonah was asked to predict: "for I know that You are a gracious and merciful God, slow to anger and abundant in lovingkindness, One who relents from doing harm" (Jonah 4:2). Some of the implementations of the Lord's judgments are contingent on resistance to, or alternatively obedience to, His call for repentance. When the response to His warning message is remorse and contrition He, in mercy, stays His hand. Clearly God can decide not to fulfill a prophecy of chastisement if people sincerely choose, from their hearts, to repent.

> Then Jeremiah spoke to all the princes and to all the people, saying, "The Lord sent me to prophesy against this house and against this city with all the words that you have heard. Now therefore amend your ways and your doings, and obey the voice of the Lord your God; then Lord will relent concerning the doom that He has pronounced against you." (Jer 26:12–13)

The question arises concerning those who never hear the gospel from the lips of a Christian. There are some helpful answers to this question, but the subject is beyond the scope of this small book. Many of God's ways concerning the worldwide ingathering of souls are beyond finding out, yet we can be certain that the extent of His work reaches far beyond anything that we could ever imagine. Nevertheless, one of the most crucial issues requiring a response from all of us who possess His written Word is the call to repent and seek God. It is definitely up to us to choose either to seek or to ignore our Creator: "And you shall seek Me, and find Me, when you seek for Me with all of your heart" (Jer 29:13). Isaiah also reminds us of this fundamental need to take the initiative and turn ourselves towards God: "Seek the Lord while He may be found, call upon Him while he is near" (Isa 55:6).

14

Does God Really Love His Enemies?
Must We Love Ours?

How could God ask us to love our enemies if, in fact, He did not love His? Concerning man's eternal well being, many Calvinists maintain that there are numerous people whom God does not love, or for whom His love is not a "love unto salvation." For them God's love can be very relative indeed. They agree that God loves His own children intensely, but does the fact that God *is* Love permeate their understanding of His feelings and dealings with man? In 1 John 4:8, we read these wonderful words: "God is love." Let us pause and allow this glorious affirmation to thrill again the depths of our hearts. God is love! J. I. Packer, a prominent Calvinist, said it so well:

> To know God's love is indeed heaven on earth. The New Testament sets forth this knowledge, not as the privilege of a favored few, but as a normal part of ordinary Christian experience, something to which only the spiritually unhealthy or malformed will be a stranger. When Paul says, "The love of God is shed abroad in our hearts by the Holy Spirit which is given to us" (Rom 5:5), he means, not love for God, as Augustine thought, but knowledge of God's love for us.[1]

Would not people who sincerely love us do all they can to help us? If we exercise Christian love towards others, we sincerely desire what is best for them. This love is just a faint reflection of how much God loves those He created. It is true that God's sovereignty, correctly defined, is one of Scripture's greatest themes, but according to His Word, the supreme characteristic of His personality and disposition is "love."

---

1. Packer, *Knowing God*, 129.

In Galatians 6:10 we find these words: "Therefore, as we have opportunity, let us do good to all, especially to those who are of the household of faith." And Jesus says in Matthew 5:44, "But I say to you, love your enemies, bless those that curse you, do good to those who hate you, and pray for those who spitefully use you and persecute you." In these verses, among many others, God exhorts us to do good to everybody, yet would God Himself do any less when it comes to the full availability of salvation to all men? As we saw earlier, some maintain that God does not love His enemies, those who habitually sin against Him, but consigns many of them to hell even before they are born, thus giving them no opportunity to become aware of their sin, repent of it, and turn to Him! Are we humans called to behave more charitably towards the lost than God would appear to behave towards them?

On the cross, Jesus prays to His Father in these significant terms: "Father, forgive them, for they do not know what they do" (Luke 23:34). Wrath and retribution are not featured here, even in the midst of such wickedness. Jesus asked for forgiveness for those who so cruelly put Him to death on the cross! What a glorious picture of mercy triumphing over judgment! Jesus, who was God incarnate, gave the perfect demonstration of loving one's enemies and He encourages us to let our lives be characterized by forgiveness and love.

Let us stop and meditate on Jesus' supreme demonstration of mercy, abstaining from any call for an outpouring of divine wrath upon His cruel torturers. We see Stephen doing this, in Acts 7:60, when at the point of death by stoning. Nevertheless, the inconceivable horrors of condemnation and hell are an ever-present reality for those who willfully, persistently, and consciously reject Christ's forgiveness and His atoning work on their behalf.

"God is Love"! Would not someone who sincerely loves us do all they can to help us? If we love others in a spiritual sense, we desire their best, and all the good that can come to them. This love is just a faint reflection of how much God loves His creatures. God can also be jealous and angry, but these are not His predominant characteristics. Incidentally, God the Father has a humble and gentle spirit, not one hungering for His own glory at the expense of helpless sinners. Jesus, who at all times personified His Father's true nature and character, and who said, "He who has seen Me has seen the Father," (John 14:9), also said, "Take My yoke upon you and learn of Me, for I am gentle and lowly in heart, and you will find rest unto your souls" (Matt 11:29). These words clearly portray the beauty of the character of the Father, whose Word also plainly testifies of His loving heart and longing to save all mankind. "And we have seen and testify that the Father sent the Son to be the Savior of the world" (1 John 4:14).

Look at what the parable of the Good Samaritan teaches us: "A certain Samaritan, as he journeyed, came where he [the injured man] was. And when he saw him he had compassion" (Luke 10:33). Jesus then says, "Go and do likewise." The Samaritans were traditional enemies of the Jews and much despised. Now would Jesus ask us to behave more honorably than His heavenly Father behaves? Of course not! If God commands us to love our enemies and do good to them, we can be certain that our God, Who is Love, does so much more than we ever could conceive towards seeking to save those who are lost. James reminds us of just how compassionate God is with those who endure and don't give up: "Indeed we count them blessed who endure. You have heard of the perseverance of Job and seen the end intended by the Lord—that the Lord is very compassionate and merciful" (Jas 5:11).

The Lord Jesus mourned over the people of Jerusalem with sorrow and yearning, making it plain that the great obstacle to their redemption was their unwillingness to let Him gather them to Himself:

> O Jerusalem, Jerusalem, the one who kills the prophets, and stones those who are sent to her! How often I wanted to gather your children together, as a hen gathers her chicks under her wings, but you were not willing. (Matt 23:37)

We can incontrovertibly translate the Greek verb in this significant declaration of Christ's as "you were not *willing*," and not as "you were not *able*." If Jesus were in fact weeping over people who had not been granted any grace to want to be gathered to Him, then would it not be a weeping of frustration because His Father in heaven was declining to reach down in mercy to help make these people willing? Do you really think this is what the passage means?

When folk in a Samaritan village declined to receive Jesus, James and John asked, "Lord, do You want us to command fire to come down from heaven and consume them, just as Elijah did" (Luke 9:54)? But He turned and rebuked them, saying, "You do not know what manner of spirit you are of. For the Son of Man did not come to destroy men's lives, but to save them" (Luke 9:55–56). Jesus' response is to re-enforce the fact that He came to save and not to destroy.

In Mark 10:21, Jesus looked with love and sadness upon the rich young man who went away sorrowing, unwilling to give up his riches. If the five points of TULIP theology were true, would not Jesus' love have overcome this young man's resistance and enabled him to respond despite himself?

From the beginning of their election, God appealed to the Israelites to choose Him over the foreign gods around them. The covenant with His special people, contracted at Sinai, is altogether a two-way transaction:

> Now therefore, if you will indeed obey My voice and keep My covenant, then you shall be a special treasure to Me above all people; for all the earth is Mine. And you shall be to Me a kingdom of priests and a holy nation. (Exod 19:5–6)

Joshua in turn emphasizes this challenge to choose obedience:

> And if it seems evil to you to serve the Lord, choose for yourselves this day whom you will serve; whether the gods which your fathers served that were on the other side of the flood, or the gods of the Amorites, in whose land you dwell. But as for me and my house, we will serve the Lord (Josh 24:15). If you forsake the Lord and serve foreign gods, then He will turn and do you harm, and consume you after He has done you good. (Josh 24:20)

Jesus, always speaks of God as His Father, and introduces Him as Father to the disciples. A good earthly father tries to treat all of his children equitably and to show no favoritism. While in Luke 15:13 the prodigal son was far away in sin, his father longed for his return and re-integration into the family circle. This younger son made a foolish choice and then hungry, dissipated, and disillusioned, he repented and returned to his loving and welcoming father. The prodigal came to himself on his own, without parental pressure or manipulation. Then when the older brother, full of resentment, stood angrily outside, the father went out to reason gently with him, without reproach. Both sons have insulted and humiliated their father, yet the father humbly seeks to be reconciled with both children. What could be simpler, clearer, and more beautiful as an illustration of how our loving heavenly Father is ready to deal with all erring sinners?

While we must be very wary of formulating doctrine from Jesus' parables, this one does not portray the father as being wrathful and offended by the son's wanderings, or irritated by the older brother's resentment. Nor did he try to stop the son from leaving. He could have, no doubt, declined to hand over the son's inheritance, but instead he sadly acquiesces in his son's decision, and refrains from controlling him, knowing this to be the only cure for his wanderlust. We are reminded in 1 John 5: 19 that "the whole world lies under the sway of the wicked one." Our heavenly Father allows many things that are not His perfect will, thus preserving our liberty of choice.

In Romans 1:18–19 we read: "For the wrath of God is revealed from heaven against all ungodliness and unrighteousness of men, who suppress the truth in unrighteousness, because what may be known of God is manifest in them, for God has shown it to them." This is not saying God directs His wrath against simply everybody, but against ungodly people who are suppressing the truth and clinging consciously to wrong ways, knowing that they contravene God's laws, as opposed to those who do seek God with sincerity, and who do not come into this category. When we read Romans 3:9–19, we need to consider it in the context of Paul's strenuous effort to expose and address the Jewish tendency to count on right standing with God through obedience to the Law, rather than upon God's mercy and the reality of one's ongoing admission of guilt and unworthiness in His presence. Paul's argument is entirely devoted to countering self-righteousness, and is not offered as proof that nobody actually seeks God, because other Scriptures make it clear that some do.

The Lord made this clear, unequivocal statement in Jeremiah 29:13: "And you will seek Me and find Me when you will search for Me with all your heart."

God's Spirit is at work in all nations, seeking to draw all men to Himself. The culmination of the conflict between good and evil is found at the cross where love triumphs over the powers of darkness. Here Jesus bears all the guilt of humanity's sin, and the demands of God's justice are forever satisfied. According to Hebrews 10:20, the way into His holy presence through the veil, His flesh, was then fully opened up for whoever chooses to go in on God's terms.

It is true that God ends up hating, in the sense of a lesser love, persistently unrepentant rebels, as in Psalm 11:5: "The Lord tests the righteous, but the wicked and the one that loves violence His soul hates." Ultimately,

God can, and does, turn even man's rebellion into victory through the cross of Christ. The Bible tells us in Romans 14:10–11 and Philippians 2:9–10 that one day every rebel knee will bow before the Risen Christ, not from a change of heart, but constrained under His authority at the judgment seat. However, we can confidently conclude that His preferred way of obtaining this victory is through the repentance and salvation of sinners, rather than a forced bowing of the knee at the judgment seat. The following verse exhorts us to love our enemies: "But I say to you, love your enemies, bless those who curse you, do good to those who hate you, and pray for those who spitefully use you and persecute you" (Matt 5:44).

Again I ask, are we humans to have a higher moral code than that of God? Of course not! We can count on the fact that God is more compassionate than we could ever imagine. His bountiful kindness and immense mercy extend over all His works: "The Lord is gracious and full of compassion, slow to anger and great in mercy. The Lord is good to all, and His tender mercies are over all His works" (Ps 145:8–9). A very comforting verse in Psalm 119:64 reinforces this sublime truth: "The earth, O Lord, is full of Your mercy."

We can count on the Lord's willingness to seek to save all who are lost. Again, this has nothing to do with universalism, the idea that eventually God will be able to save everybody who has ever lived. The Lord of creation is even now giving all people, except those who have hardened their hearts beyond remedy, the opportunity of repenting and seeking Him. "God was in Christ reconciling the world to Himself, not imputing their trespasses to them, and has committed unto us the word of reconciliation" (2 Cor 5:19). It is a tragic theological error to try to make such statements as these mean anything less than that our all-loving God opens up the way of reconciliation to all men. Colossians 1:20 further confirms God's intent: "and by Him to reconcile all things to Himself, by Him, whether things on earth or things in heaven, having made peace through the blood of His cross." The following verses bring us back to the heart of the gospel message:

> And as Moses lifted up the serpent in the wilderness, even so must the Son of Man be lifted up, that whoever believes in Him should not perish but have eternal life. For God so loved the world that He gave His only begotten Son, that whoever believes in Him should not perish, but have everlasting life. For God did not send His Son

into the world to condemn the world, but that the world through Him might be saved. (John 3:14–17)

Now the only limitation we can legitimately place upon the "all things" and "whosoever" in the above verse is the clear light from other Scriptures that fallen angels have already forfeited any opportunity to repent and turn back to God. They possessed the full knowledge and vision of God and yet chose to rebel. Satan and demons will therefore be inexorably cast into the lake of fire and brimstone, which was initially prepared for them, and not originally for human beings. "Then the King will turn to those on the left and say, 'Away with you, you cursed ones, into the eternal fire prepared for the devil and his angels (Matt 25:41). It was never God's desire or original intent to cast any human being into that terrible lake. Choosing consciously and definitively to cling to rebellion, a sin against the Holy Spirit, is the true and only cause of this eternal punishment, because by so doing one has forever sided with Satan and his demons.

Incidentally, one can profitably study throughout Scripture the references to "whoever" and "whosoever." In the following Scriptures they are inclusive words, denoting an indiscriminate and generous attitude towards humanity. Notice the family bond with Jesus that is established when we set out to accomplish God's will: "For whosoever does the will of My Father in Heaven is My brother and sister and mother" (Matt 12:50). Provided we are faithful in the small things, the Lord stands by to grant more: "For whoever has, to him more will be given, and he will have abundance; but whoever does not have, even what he has will be taken away from him" (Matt 13:12). However, if we remain self-centered, we will tragically lose out: "For whoever desires to save his life will lose it, but whoever loses his life for My sake will find it" (Matt 16:25). The surest, safest way to proceed is to genuinely humble ourselves before the Lord: "Therefore whoever humbles himself as this little child is the greatest in the Kingdom of Heaven" (Matt 18:4). There can be no doubt at all that if we choose to call upon Him, He will deliver us: "And it shall come to pass that whoever calls on the name of the Lord shall be saved" (Acts 2:21).

In the light of all the previously mentioned quotes, does it make sense that we could justifiably approach God with any doubt in our spirit about His love for us, fearful that we might be one of those whom He had chosen not to love? We are commanded to love everybody because, basically, God Himself loves everybody and desires the very best for each of us.

15

Does Everyone Have Faith?

THERE ARE VERY FREQUENT everyday situations where we exercise confidence, trust, and faith. Trust, unless parents betray it, develops in offspring during infancy, and this confidence in parents is instinctive in small children. We normally have faith in people and situations from the moment we awake in the morning. We do not ask for proof that our breakfast cereals contain no deadly poison; we trust the manufacturer. We trust ourselves to our vehicles, whether or not we have any real understanding of how they work. We have faith in each other in the workplace, that each will get on with his respective task for the good of the company. We all already possess this natural ability to exercise confidence, trust, and faith, the three of which for all practical purposes are synonymous in everyday life.

With respect to faith, a most interesting episode in Peter's life occurs when the disciples see Jesus walking on the water towards their boat:

> And Peter answered Him and said, "Lord, if it is You, command me to come to You on the water." So He said, "Come" And when Peter had come down out of the boat, he walked on the water to go to Jesus. But when he saw that the wind was boisterous, he was afraid; and beginning to sink he cried out, saying, "Lord, save me!" And immediately Jesus stretched out His hand and caught him, and said to him, "O you of little faith, why did you doubt?" (Matt 14:28–31)

Now if exercising faith were an ability exclusively given only to selected people, surely Jesus would have said something like this to Peter: "Dear Peter, I'm so sorry. You sank because I forgot to give you the faith and irresistible grace to keep looking at Me." We see that Jesus was often saddened by how little faith His own disciples exercised, as when He calmed the storm on the Sea of Galilee. He asks them, "Why are you so fearful, O you of little faith? Then He rose and rebuked the winds and the sea, and there was a great calm" (Matt 8:26). Here is more proof that Jesus expected them to exercise the innate faith that they already possessed.

In Mark 6:5 we read: "Now He could do no mighty works there, except that He laid His hands on a few sick folk, and healed them. And He marveled because of their unbelief." Jesus also marveled in Matthew 8:10, at the centurion's faith. Why would Jesus be so surprised to see faith being exercised by one person, and saddened by its absence in another, if faith itself was exclusively an ability or quality that He distributed according to His own selective will? The truth is that we can choose to direct this general type of faith, trust, confidence, belief (all closely related words) towards seeking God, and in doing so can develop "saving faith" as God meets us according to His promise, "Seek and you shall find" (Matt 7:7). The alternative is to neglect or refuse to do so with tragic results as we bow to other gods, such as materialism, prestige, or any number of other pursuits.

The Word of God constantly exhorts both Christians and unbelievers to believe in God and His promises. Regarding the following verse: "For by grace you have been saved through faith, and that not of yourselves; it is the gift of God" (Eph 2:8), the gift of God mentioned here refers to the subject of the preceding verses in Ephesians, that is to say to the whole package of salvation and not to "faith" alone. In his commentary on Ephesians chapter 2, John Calvin rightly said that it referred to salvation in all its aspects and not just to faith. The word "faith" is feminine in Greek but the word "that" is neuter, so it cannot be referring just to "faith."

Thus faith does not denote some mysterious ability bestowed by God on a select few, but a faculty that, in essence, we already have the ability to exercise. God invites us to ask Him to help our faith to grow. Biblical faith is simply exercising trust in what God says and what He has done for us. When the Word says, in Hebrews 11:6, that "without faith it is impossible to please Him, for he who comes to God must believe that He is and that He is a rewarder of those who diligently seek Him," it means that until we choose to trust in Him with our whole being, we have no real confidence in Him and bring Him no true pleasure. The word "faith" in Scripture implies trust in God. The Lord Jesus is of course eager to help us increase our faith, and we can ask Him to do so, just as the disciples did in Luke 17:5: "And the apostles said to the Lord, 'Increase our faith.'" He often answers this cry from our hearts by testing the faith we have, and allowing trials and tribulations so that we truly cry out to Him in desperation, with a sense of our own helplessness and inadequacy.

There is such a generous and encouraging invitation to us all found in Revelation 22:17: "And the Spirit and the bride say, 'Come.' Let him who hears say, 'Come.' And let him that is athirst come. And whoever will, let him take the water of life freely." Is this invitation from the Spirit of God sincere towards all? Yes, the glorious truth is that every one of us possesses the potential to choose to place our faith in the Lord, Jesus Christ. It really is up to us to go to Him; the invitation is there, and we are all free to approach Him, just like those who approached Him during His earthly ministry. "In the last day, that great day of the feast, Jesus stood and cried, saying,

> "If any man thirst, let him come to Me, and drink. He who believes on Me, as the Scripture says, out of his innermost being shall flow rivers of living water." But this He spoke of the Spirit, whom those that believe on Him would receive: for the Holy Spirit was not yet given; because Jesus was not yet glorified. (John 7:37–39)

The invitation to be saved is sent out to the farthest corners of the earth. In Isaiah 45:22, we read: "Look unto Me, and be saved, all the ends of the earth: for I am God, and there is none else." This would be a deceptive invitation indeed, if the call to be saved were confined just to Israel, or some other specific group. In reality, this is a wonderful call going out to everybody on earth, without distinction of race, age, color, or even the creed in which they were raised. "For the grace of God that brings salvation has appeared to all men" (Titus 2:11). How could this possibly mean that God's grace is limited? We can rest in the assurance that the wonderful grace of God is worldwide in scope and that His immense mercy will triumph over judgment. According to Revelation 5:9, souls will be present in heaven from every language and tribe on earth, yet as far as we know some tribes have become extinct without being evangelized by Christians. The scope of God's redemptive work is unmistakably far greater than we can ever imagine.

Jesus says, "Whoever wishes, let him take the free gift of the water of life" (Rev 22:17 NIV). Would Jesus say, "whoever wishes, let him take," if He was only inviting "those to whom the Father had granted faith" to take of it? As always, we can count on Jesus to say exactly what He means to say! It is patently clear that it is our responsibility to exercise faith and heed the voice of God:

> But My people would not heed My voice, and Israel would have none of Me. Therefore, I gave them up to their own hearts' lust, and they walked in their own counsels. Oh that My people would listen to Me, and Israel would walk in My ways! (Ps 81:11–13)

Look again at Jesus' disciples, and the fact that He was so often surprised by their lack of faith, as stated in Matthew 16:8: "But when Jesus perceived this, He said unto them, 'O you of little faith, why do you reason among yourselves, because you have brought no bread?'" Would Jesus express surprise at the disciples' degree of faith if in fact it were He who gave such faith in the first place? Clearly, as in Hebrews 11:1, faith is not primarily some "substance" that Jesus imparts, but a capacity to trust that we already possess and that we must choose to activate and direct towards the Lord. Let us assure ourselves of this glorious truth: our Heavenly Father is eager to encourage and strengthen our faith as we wait upon Him.

16

What Is the Perseverance of the Saints, according to TULIP?

AMONG TULIP PROPONENTS, THERE are many who say that the only reason we Christians ever persevere is because God has chosen to "dose" us with some special disposition, coming entirely from Him, which makes us plod on in life, and eventually reach our everlasting rest with Him in heaven, all because of His doing, for His glory alone. However, is this true? Is there no place for genuine human qualities of perseverance, apart from this special dose of grace from God? Calvinists say that once we are saved we can never be lost because of God, and only because of Him. However, is this what the Scriptures really say? Hebrews 3:6 openly states that we go on belonging to God's house only if we choose to "hold fast the confidence and the rejoicing of the hope firm to the end."

The Bible does indeed teach that we can enjoy assurance of salvation and be eternally secure, but not primarily because of some divine decree as expressed in the fifth point of TULIP. Resting our assurance on some real or supposed divine election can easily create a spirit of uncertainty. How can I be really sure that God elected me? Satan is a vicious accuser of God's children and their failures can lead some Calvinists to question if they really do belong to the elect. Other Christians can also be plunged into total despair, fearing that their sin has caused them to lose their salvation.

Jesus tells us explicitly that our security is assured if we truly belong to His flock: "My sheep hear My voice, and I know them and they follow Me. And I give them eternal life, and they shall never perish, neither shall anyone snatch them out of My hand" (John 10:27). This is a very encouraging and clear statement, and all other Scripture statements need to be interpreted in the light of this precious and unequivocal promise made by Jesus to His own sheep:

> They shall never perish. (John 10:28)

Let us notice that Jesus did not say, "My sheep *heard* My voice." What happened in the past is important, but listening to Him today is even more so. What marvelous comfort, what positive assurance, for those who have truly entrusted their lives to Jesus! And to those who despair of ever making it in their own strength, we can state confidently that people who daily nurture a spirit of repentance and childlike trust can enjoy a strong sense of being eternally secure. Such a true disciple is one who is fully committed to the Lord Jesus Christ, denying self and taking up his cross daily, seeking to obey the Lord and eager to grow in Christlikeness.

What, then, are the proofs that one truly belongs to His flock? Firstly, Jesus says that His sheep hear His voice. He does not say, "My sheep know the Scriptures," important as it is to apply oneself to hiding God's Word in one's heart, as in Psalm 119:10. Many scribes and Pharisees knew the Scriptures without wanting to follow Jesus. His true sheep actively depend on their Shepherd for their sustenance and their entire well-being. We need daily to ask ourselves if our heart is truly open to the gentle voice of our Shepherd, eager to be guided by Him during the day, learning to live in intimate contact with our Protector and Guide. All too easily, the solicitations of the world, the flesh, and the devil drown out the voice of Jesus. Secondly, Jesus added that His sheep follow Him. Let us notice the present tense, not "followed" but "follow." His genuine sheep go on following and will not listen to false shepherds. The sheep follow Him, for they know His voice.

> The sheep hear His voice; and He calls His own sheep by name and leads them out. And when He brings out His own sheep, He goes before them; and the sheep follow Him, for they know His voice. Yet they will by no means follow a stranger, but will flee from him, for they do not know the voice of strangers. (John 10:3–5)

Then there are other tests of true discipleship, most importantly the practice of love towards other believers: "By this all will know that you are My disciples, if you have love for one another" (John 13:35). Our love for our brothers in Christ is a vital sign of spiritual life. How tragic that love is sometimes lacking amongst Christians!

> We know that we have passed from death unto life, because we love the brethren. He who does not love his brother abides in death. Whoever hates his brother is a murderer, and you know that no murderer has eternal life abiding in him. By this we know love, because He laid down His life for us. And we also ought to lay down our lives for the brethren. (1 John 3:14–16)

What is our true inward attitude towards our neighbors and fellow-Christians? This question is incredibly important! Does one habitually put one's own needs before those of others? Doing so need not mean one is not a Christian. It may just mean one still has a lot of growing to do. Look at how the apostle Paul felt about the Jews who persecuted Him: "I tell the truth in Christ, I am not lying, my conscience also bearing me witness in the Holy Spirit, that I have great sorrow and continual grief in my heart. For I could wish that I myself were accursed from Christ for my brethren, my countrymen according to the flesh" (Rom 9:1–3). Are we ready to die for our neighbors, or do we ignore them, or resent them, or let ourselves get too busy to come alongside when they need us?

Let the parable of the sower speak to us on the subject. There are those who receive the Word with real joy, but who, like seeds upon a rock, develop no solid roots. They just give cerebral or emotional acquiescence: "But the ones on the rock are those who, when they hear, receive the word with joy; and these have no root, who believe for a while, and in time of temptation fall away" (Luke 8:13).

One can easily receive the Word yet lack depth, growing only for a short time before drifting back into the world. Tragically, one can also accept the Word without allowing it to transform the heart and change the inner disposition, and thus fail to reorient the whole focus of one's aspirations and goals. The Word of God does not expressly say either that we cannot abandon Him through our own willful disobedience, plucking ourselves out of His hand, though it would appear inconceivable to me that anybody would want to turn his back on the Lord Jesus once he has truly come to know Him. How could one choose to go back into darkness and death from the light and safety of our Shepherd's fold?

In addition to the assurance given by the Scriptures, if we truly belong to Him we also have a powerful testimony concerning our eternal security implanted in our hearts by the Holy Spirit: "The Spirit itself bears witness with our spirit that we are children of God" (Rom 8:16). We need to note the emphasis John put on an inner testimony in our heart: "He that believes in the Son of God has the witness in himself" (1 John 5:10). "Belief," in this verse, implies relying on God in everyday matters. We cannot live our lives with Christ unless He in turn lives out His life within us: "By this we know that we abide in Him, and He in us, because He has given us of his Spirit" (1 John 4:13). When we walk in the light as His obedient sons and daughters, our inner spirit keeps reminding us of our marvelous status as His own children. Furthermore, you cannot live in God's love without also loving all other Christians: "We know that we have passed from death unto life, because we love the brethren. He that does not love his brother abides in death" (1 John 3:14).

Additionally Jesus, always our best authority, stated that, in order to attain the goal, we must persevere and endure to the end: "But he who endures to the end will be saved" (Matt 24:13). The following statement reinforces this truth: "For we have become partakers of Christ, if we hold the beginning of our confidence steadfast to the end" (Heb 3:14).

Clearly, salvation is more than just an event, or a decision, since it involves an ongoing disposition of putting aside self-effort, and embracing the way of repentance, submission, and obedience to our precious Lord in the power of the Holy Spirit. The real Christian life is a relationship of love with our marvelous Savior. His authentic sheep persevere in their relationship with Him, trusting in the astounding goodness, grace, and mercy of their Shepherd who will never abandon them.

Many make the mistake of thinking that the significant act of "making a decision for Christ" in an evangelistic campaign sufficiently guarantees their good standing with God. Of course, this decision can indeed represent a profound change from death to life, from the realm of darkness to the kingdom of light. However, our salvation is so much more than simply an intellectual assent to certain facts, or an emotional response to persuasive preaching. True conversion involves a profound encounter with the risen Christ. One can faithfully attend church services and meetings, and enjoy much of what the company of believers has to offer, yet not be truly part of the redeemed community.

The question seems to hang upon whether we are genuinely "in Christ" as distinct from having had some religious experience, however intense: "Therefore, if anyone is in Christ, he is a new creation; old things have passed away; behold, all things have become new" (2 Cor 5:17).

In Acts 14:22 we see Paul and Barnabas exhorting the disciples in Lystra, Iconium, and Antioch "to continue in the faith." We must allow such texts to speak for themselves and not try to explain away their plain meaning in order to fit our own theological position. Through unbelief and carelessness we can fall away from submission to God, and become backsliders needing to repent and be restored to close communion with our Lord.

Our true spiritual disposition is also revealed by our attitude to the Scriptures. Do we try to squeeze the texts into our own pre-conceived doctrinal and moral notions, rather than allowing the Scriptures to judge us? Jesus' true sheep seek to approach the Word with deep respect, and submit to its teaching without trying to adapt or modify it to fit their situation. Those who dissect and cut up the Holy Word of God are in great danger. We are not called upon to judge the Word, but to let it judge us. A good indication of being on the right road is that we approach the Scriptures fully eager to be corrected by them, and allowing them to stimulate our own heart, without attempting to alter the text to suit our own beliefs and justify our less than Christlike behavior.

Being saved from our sins is not an event but a relationship, sincerely and truthfully nurtured as a life of dependence upon God through His Holy Spirit, by whom we cry "Abba, Father," and who "bears witness with our spirit that we are children of God" (Rom 8:15–16).

Nowhere does the Bible actually use the words "Once saved, always saved," and a good reason for this would be that God wants us to draw our reassurance from more than one source. As already mentioned, there is, in addition to the written Word, the inner witness of the Holy Spirit. Remember, the scribes, Sadducees, and Pharisees were very well versed in the Scriptures, yet most became Christ's fiercest adversaries, even using the very words of Scripture to oppose Him. This fact is extremely prominent in the Gospels, serving as a most solemn warning to us not to base our assurance on Bible texts alone. We must let the Holy Spirit apply the Word to our hearts and circumstances, giving us the assurance of where we stand in our relationship to God.

As we have said, it is inconceivable that a true member of Christ's flock would ever want to stop trusting in Him. However, so strong is the pull of the world, and so subtle the subterfuges of Satan, that we who follow the Lord need every incentive and admonition against backsliding, to avoid complacency and self-righteous stances. We can learn from what God said to the Gentiles regarding Israel, although the context is national rather than individual. The lesson is vital: deal with pride, and cultivate reverent fear of God. "For if God did not spare the natural branches, He may not spare you either. Therefore consider the goodness and severity of God: on those, who fell, severity; but toward you, goodness, if you continue in His goodness. Otherwise, you also will be cut off" (Rom 11:21–22).

If the Word of God seems to warn us about the possibility of falling away, where then can we get the comfort and assurance of eternal life that make us feel secure? In practice, eternal security is less a matter of quoting proof texts than of this inner witness implanted by the Holy Spirit. A good way to experience a deep sense of the reality of eternal security is to cultivate a heart of worship and praise, and to walk in a spirit that repudiates self-confidence and self-righteousness, but nurtures instead a repentant spirit. Repentance is much more an ongoing exercise of heart and mind than just an essential element in our conversion itself. The seven churches mentioned in Revelation chapter 3 were noted, with the exception of Smyrna and Philadelphia, as needing a renewed experience of repentance. Hebrews 6:1 speaks of repentance as part of the foundation rather than part of the scaffolding. You can remove scaffolding without necessarily threatening the stability of a building, but what happens if you remove the foundation?

Repentance is needful in our daily walk with the Lord, so let us avoid the danger of complacently seeing repentance as something that is over and dealt with in our past, when it needs to continue to be a vital component of our everyday experience of walking with God.

There are strong descriptive words in Hebrews 6:4–8 which particularly challenge us; words like "enlightened," "tasted the heavenly gift," "become partakers of the Holy Spirit," and "tasted the good word of God and the powers of the world to come." However, these phrases do not necessarily describe someone who has fully committed his life to Jesus Christ, and received Him as Savior and Lord. Nevertheless, we all need to examine our heart and take very seriously all the warnings found in the Word of God, not tolerating in ourselves any carelessness in spiritual matters. In the same epistle, we have this solemn admonition: "Beware brethren, lest there be in any of you an evil heart of unbelief, in departing from the living God" (Heb 3:12). Paul exhorts us to "Examine yourselves to see whether you are in the faith; test yourselves" (2 Cor 13:5). Complacency and carelessness must be forever forsaken.

What are we to make of the warning in Revelation 22:19: "And if any one take from the words of the book of this prophecy, God will take away his part from the tree of life, and out of the holy city, which are written in this book?" How could God remove someone's part in the tree of life, unless up to that point he had it? It seems to me that the best answer to this is that all true disciples do not tamper with the inspiration and completeness of the Word of God, but constantly nurture a deep and abiding respect for all of the Bible, and put aside regular times to study it closely.

SO WHAT IS THE SIN AGAINST THE HOLY SPIRIT?

The sin against the Holy Spirit is not some specific deed, however appalling, but rather a persistent attitude of the heart. Jesus explained that He could forgive all manner of sins except this one sin against the Holy Spirit. It appears that the sin against the Holy Spirit was, first of all, attributing Jesus' work to the devil, as did the Pharisees in Matthew 12:24. Today, since the sacrifice of Jesus on the cross, we can take it to include the attitude of persistent, definitive refusal to heed God's voice and benefit from Christ's redemptive sacrifice on our behalf, turning one's back on Him and thus spurning the only source of eternal life. Taking this stand would be like saying that individuals could bypass the cross and accomplish their own salvation, believing in the false offer of "another way," and effectively traveling the road to ultimate damnation. People thus condemn themselves to a lost eternity by constant neglect and persistent rebellion against the Lord.

It is not God's will that any of us perish. Hell was prepared for the devil and his angels, not for men. (See Matthew 25:41.) However, taking the road offered by Satan, and closing one's ears and heart to God, will result in following him to that awful place. God longs for all people everywhere to repent. Of course he does!

There are some very clear warnings in Scripture concerning eternal separation from God. Only God can absolutely see into our hearts and show us whether we have set our heart upon obedience or rebellion.
If we discern in our own heart and mind a clear resolve to please God, then we can be sure that we have not committed the sin against the Holy Spirit.

It takes time and suffering to become like Jesus, and we will often stumble in the process, repeatedly picking ourselves up again, and carrying on with the grace and help offered by our loving God. Undoubtedly our old sin nature will continue to cause us significant inner distress all of our life. However, the wonderful thing is that we are no longer under sin's dominion and a glorious future awaits us, where sin will no longer be present. Hallelujah! Such distress is a very positive sign of our being on the right road. People who have committed the sin against the Holy Spirit have no genuine concern at all for the things of God.

17

How Then Should We Respond to God's Love?

THE VIEWS WE HAVE been countering redefine God's sovereignty so that man's genuine, autonomous freedom of choice, in the sense that ordinary people understand freedom, is denied and God's great love for all mankind is narrowed in its scope. TULIP views are part of what are often called "the doctrines of grace." Would you now agree that a truer description of those ideas would be "the doctrines of condemnation?" Calvin himself tended to pour scorn on all who disagreed with him, and much of the way he sought to rule Geneva constituted a clear case of spiritual abuse. Amongst so much that is excellent in his teaching, it is vitally important that we challenge and expose the false elements and the consequent wrong interpretations and attitudes that have caused great distress and division in many churches.

At the conclusion of the Council of Dordrecht, the Calvinist party began to persecute severely those who disagreed with their position on election and man's free will. Many dissenting pastors were defrocked, some servants of God were executed, and others exiled. What a lamentable outcome among those on both sides who held so many basic doctrines in common, like the true divinity and humanity of our Lord Jesus Christ! The Calvinist party became the persecutors of their dissenting brethren!

Our incentive to share the good news is reinforced by the following assurance: Nobody we ever meet has been excluded from God's mercy solely by some divine decree.

What joy there is in telling others that Jesus loves them and died for all their sins! What folly to imagine that we can love somebody that God had decided from eternity past not to love! Imagine approaching a person and saying, "Look, God has predestined millions of people to hell. I would just like to find out if you happen to be numbered amongst them?" If ever we said something similar to an unsaved person, a normal response would be "Is that so? Okay, you can keep your God to yourself. I want nothing to do with that kind of deity."

We can all become effective ambassadors and workers together with God in sharing the good news that Jesus died for humanity's sins, exercising the ministry of reconciliation that has been committed to us in the spirit of the following verse: "Now all things are of God, who has reconciled us to Himself through Jesus Christ, and has given us the ministry of reconciliation" (2 Cor 5:18). Such is the desire of His loving heart.

Supremely, the Bible reveals to us God's heart of love: "May the Lord direct your hearts into the love of God, and into patient waiting for Christ" (2 Thess 3:5). We find this same emphasis on God's kindness and love in so many other places, such as Titus 3:4–6: "But after the kindness and love of God our Savior toward man appeared, not by works of righteousness which we have done, but according to His mercy He saved us, by the washing of regeneration, and renewing of the Holy Ghost, which He shed on us abundantly through Jesus Christ our Savior." His sovereignty, rightly understood, is peculiarly His own and something we do not share in, although we greatly benefit from it, whereas His love is something we do participate in, and pass on to a suffering world.

God's sovereignty is one of Scripture's greatest themes, but the love of God, not His sovereignty, is the cardinal theme of Scripture. We are ambassadors of His kingdom of love and light in this darkened world, and we can shine forth the visible reality of the fullness of His presence within us: "And to know the love of Christ, which passes knowledge, that you might be filled with all the fullness of God" (Eph 3:19). There is in fact only one gospel, the good news that Jesus died for all men, revealing the Father's great heart of love.

If we meet fellow believers who have not yet grasped these enlightening truths, let us beware of becoming aggressive, but, rather, keep our testimony shining in a spirit of gentleness and love. Let us treat them with respect and demonstrate the love of which we speak. Believers, whose convictions differ from ours, certainly need to face the facts we have presented, and ask themselves if their understanding of God's dealings with man genuinely concur with the whole tenor of Scripture.

We will be overjoyed if those holding the belief that God has only predestined certain people to inherit eternal life will stop to reconsider their viewpoint in the light of the clear statements of Scripture we have sought to present. As expressed in John 3:16–17, God loves everybody in the world so much that He gave His only Son, that whosoever believes in Him should not perish, but have everlasting life. He did not send His Son to earth to condemn and judge, but to save the world through Him.

"But you, beloved, building up yourselves on your most holy faith, praying in the Holy Spirit, keep yourselves in the love of God, looking for the mercy of our Lord Jesus Christ unto eternal life" (Jude 1:20–21). Amen!

Appendix

Additional significant Scripture passages:

Introduction

"But the wisdom that is from above is first pure, then peaceable, gentle, willing to yield, full of mercy and good fruits, without partiality and without hypocrisy" (Jas 3:17).

"But we were gentle among you, just as a nursing mother cherishes her children" (1 Thess 2:7).

"To speak evil of no one, to be peaceable, gentle, showing all humility unto all men" (Titus 3:2).

"Now I, Paul, myself am pleading with you by the meekness and gentleness of Christ" (2 Cor 10:1).

"But the fruit of the Spirit is love, joy, peace, longsuffering kindness, goodness, faithfulness" (Gal 5:22–23).

Chapter 1

"He answered and said to them, 'Because it has been given to you to know the mysteries of the kingdom of heaven, but to them it has not been given'" (Matt 13:11).

Chapter 3

"I made myself gardens and orchards, and I planted all kinds of fruit trees in them" (Eccl 2:5).

"Pray in the Spirit on all occasions with all kinds of prayers" (Eph 6:18 KJV).

"The kingdom of heaven is like a dragnet that was cast into the sea and gathered some of every kind of fish" (Matt 13:47).

"Be on your guard against all kinds of greed" (Luke 12:15 KJV).

"In it were all kinds of four-footed animals" (Acts 10:12).

"Devoting herself to all kinds of good deeds" (1 Tim 5:10 KJV).

"Every kind of beast" (Jas 3:7).

"All kinds of trials" (1 Pet 1:6 KJV).

"Do not be carried away by all kinds of strange teachings" (Heb 13:9 KJV).

"And the Spirit and the bride say, 'Come!' And let him who hears say, 'Come!' And let him who thirsts come. Whoever desires, let him take the water of life freely" (Rev 22:17).

Chapter 7

"For the Son of Man did not come to destroy men's lives, but to save them" (Luke 9:56)

"Come to me, all you who labor and are heavy laden, and I will give you rest" (Matt 11:28).

"Let the wicked forsake his way and the unrighteous man his thoughts; let him return unto the Lord, and He will have mercy upon him, and to our God, for He will abundantly pardon" (Isa 55:7).

"The Lord is with you while you are with Him. If you seek Him, He will be found by you; but if you forsake Him, He will forsake you" (2 Chr 15:2).

"As for you, my son Solomon, know the God of your father, and serve Him with a loyal heart and with a willing mind; for the Lord searches all hearts and understands all the intents of the thoughts. If you seek Him, He will be found by you; but if you forsake Him, He will cast you off forever" (1 Chr 28:9).

Chapter 10

"For by Him all things were created that are in heaven, and that are on earth, visible and invisible, whether thrones, or dominions, or principalities, or powers. All things were created through Him, and for Him" (Col 1:16).

"To the intent that now the manifold wisdom of God might be made known by the church to the principalities and powers in the heavenly places" (Eph 3:10).

"Having disarmed principalities and powers, He made a public spectacle of them, triumphing over them in it" (Col 2:15).

"So rend your heart, and not your garments, return to the Lord your God; for He is gracious and merciful, slow to anger, and of great kindness, and He relents from doing harm. Who knows if He will turn and relent, and leave a blessing behind Him" (Joel 2:13–14)?

"For if you return to the Lord, your brethren and your children will be treated with compassion by those who lead them captive, so that they may come back to this land, for the Lord your God is gracious and merciful, and will not turn away His face from you if you return to Him" (2 Chr 30:9).

"Yet from the days of your fathers, you have gone away from My ordinances and have not kept them. 'Return unto Me, and I will return unto you,' says the Lord of hosts" (Mal 3:7).

"'Wash yourselves, make yourselves clean, put away the evil of your doings from before My eyes. Cease to do evil, learn to do good. Seek justice, rebuke the oppressor; defend the fatherless, plead for the widow. Come now, and let us reason together,' says the Lord. 'Though your sins are like scarlet, they shall be as white as snow; though they are red like crimson, they shall be as wool. If you are willing and obedient, you shall eat the good of the land; but if you refuse and rebel, you shall be devoured with the sword'; for the mouth of the Lord has spoken it" (Isa 1:16–20).

"And when you saw that Nahash king of the Ammonites came against you, you said to me, 'No, but a king shall reign over us,' when the Lord your God was your king. Now therefore, here is the king whom you have chosen and whom you have desired. And take note, the Lord has set a king over you. If you fear the Lord and serve Him and obey His voice, and do not rebel against the commandment of the Lord, then both you and the king who reigns over you will continue following the Lord your God. However, if you do not obey the voice of the Lord, but rebel against the commandment of the Lord, then the hand of the Lord will be against you, as it was against your fathers" (1 Sam 12:12–15).

Chapter 13

"For you, Lord, are good and ready to forgive, and abundant in mercy to all those who call upon You" (Ps 86:5).

"For the Lord is good, His mercy is everlasting; and His truth endures to all generations" (Ps 100:5).

"But the mercy of the Lord is from everlasting to everlasting on those who fear Him, and His righteousness to children's children" (Ps 103:17).

"For Your mercy is great above the heavens, and Your truth reaches to the clouds" (Ps 108:4).

"Help me, O Lord my God! Oh save me according to Your mercy" (Ps 109:26).

"The Lord is gracious and full of compassion, slow to anger and great in mercy" (Ps 145:8).

Chapter 14

"Therefore, since a promise remains of entering His rest, let us fear lest any of you seem to have come short of it. For indeed the gospel was preached to us as well as to them; but the word which they heard did not profit them, not being mixed with faith in those who heard it" (Heb 4:1–2).

Bibliography

Boettner, Lorraine. *The Reformed Doctrine of Predestination*. Eerdmans, 1932.

Broadbent, E. H. *The Pilgrim Church*. Pickering & Inglis, 1935.

Butler, Samuel. *Hudibras*. Part III, Canto III, lines 547–48. Online: http://www.exclassics.com/hudibras/hbiii3.htm.

Calvin, John. *Commentary on Genesis*. Vol. 1. Translation edited by Henry Beveridge, 1845–46. The Edinburgh Printing Company, 1857.

———. *Commentary on the Gospel of John*. Vol. 1. Translation edited by Henry Beveridge, 1845–46. The Edinburgh Printing Company, 1857.

———. *Commentaries on Timothy etc*. Translation edited by Henry Beveridge, 1845–46. The Edinburgh Printing Company, 1856.

———. *Commentary on Romans*. Translation edited by Henry Beveridge, 1845–46. The Edinburgh Printing Company, 1845.

———. *Institutes of the Christian Religion*. Translation edited by Henry Beveridge, 1845–46. Online: http://www.ccel.org/ccel/calvin/institutes.html.

Carron, T. W. *The Christian Testimony through the Ages*. Pickering & Inglis, 1957.

The English-Greek Reverse Interlinear New Testament. General editor, John Schwandt. Compiled by Logos Research Systems, 2006.

Estep, William R. *The Anabaptist Story*. Eerdmans, 1963.

Henry, Carl F. H. *God, Revelation, and Authority*. Vol. VI. Crossway Books, 1999.

Holy Bible. New International Version. New York International Bible Society, 1978.

Holy Bible. New King James Version. Thomas Nelson Publishers, 1982.

Holy Bible. New King James Version. Revised edition. Thomas Nelson Publishers, 1985.

Hunt, Dave. *What Love is This?* Loyal Publishing Inc., 2002.

Ironside, H. A. *A Historical Sketch of the Brethren Movement*. Loizeaux Brothers, 1985.

MacDonald, William. *Believer's Bible Commentary, New Testament*. Thomas Nelson Publishers, 1989.

MacLaren, Alexander. *Exposition of Holy Scripture: The Acts*. No Pages. Accessed April 28, 2008. Online: http://www.ccel.org/ccel/maclaren/acts.html.

Marston, Paul, and Roger Forster. *God's Strategy in Human History*. Wipf and Stock Publishers, 2000.

Olson, Roger E. *The Story of Christian Theology*. InterVarsity Press, 1999.

Packer, J. I. *Knowing God*. Hodder & Stoughton, 1973.

Pink, Arthur W. *The Sovereignty of God*. 4th edition. Sovereign Grace Publishers, 1949.

Pinnock, Clark H. *A Wideness in God's Mercy*. Zondervan Publishing House, 1992.

Robertson, A. T. *Word Pictures in the New Testament*. Broadman Press, 1960.

Schaff, Philip. *The History of the Christian Church*. Online: http://www.ccel.org/s/schaff/history/About.htm.

Sproul, R. C. *Chosen By God*. Tyndale House Publishers, 1994.

Bibliography

————. *Essential Truths of the Christian Faith.* Tyndale House Publishers, 1998.

Spurgeon, C. H. *Faith's Check Book.* Whitaker House, 1992.

————. *Sermons of C. H. Spurgeon.* Pilgrim Publications. Online: http://www.spurgeon .org/index.cindex.htm.

Vance, Lawrence. *The Other Side of Calvinism.* Vance Publications, 1999.

Verduin, Leonard. *The Reformers and their Stepchildren.* Eerdmans, 1964.

Vine, W. E. *Expository Dictionary of Old and New Testament Words.* Thomas Nelson Publishers, 1997.

Webster's New World Dictionary of the American Language. College Edition. World Publishing Company, 1964.

White, James. *The Potter's Freedom.* Calvary Press, 2000.

Williams, George H. *The Radical Reformation.* Westminster Press, 1962.